Many Moons Ago

Poems by

Bruno Cavazos

ISBN 978-1-64299-468-1 (paperback)
ISBN 978-1-64299-469-8 (digital)

Christian Faith Publishing, Inc.
832 Park Avenue
Meadville, PA 16335
www.christianfaithpublishing.com

Printed in the United States of America

Acknowledgments

This book is dedicated to my grandson, Gabriel Asencio Cavazos, who, at a very early age, was diagnosed with autism. We have witnessed the trials that Gabe goes through and continues to go through on a daily basis. It was this close interaction with my grandson that prompted some of my poetry. Gabe turned fourteen on March 6, 2018.

I also want to compliment Gabe's daddy (Bruno Cavazos III) and Gabe's mommy (Staci Rogers Cavazos) for their unwavering support and love afforded to my grandson. They are true examples of what proper parenting should be. They lead by example as they fully realize that this child of theirs needs all the positive reinforcement, guidance, help, encouragement, support, and love that they can and must constantly give.

As stated above, Gabe inspired some of my work, but I would also say that I was inspired by other "special needs children" and their wonderful and caring parents gathered at a local bowling alley to watch their respective child attempt to master a bowling game. I can still see the camaraderie and positive atmosphere that the parents projected while encouraging their child to do good. Claps were loudly heard for effort placed forward than for results gained. It was truly amazing to have witnessed such strong, caring, and loving parents respecting and encouraging, not only their own, but also the children of others.

Those of us that have a weak and caring heart cry inwardly and feel compassionate for these children and parents. Those of us that do not see the plight that these children and parents go through on a daily basis need to remove the plank from their eye and truly consider how their life would have been impacted if they had to care and raise a special needs child.

My salute and my deepest profound thanks to all these parents that chose pro life and on a daily basis show how to be a great and proud parent!

In closing here is an excerpt from one of the poems titled, "Strength," and sent with the utmost respect to the parents of special needs children or a loved one being cared for:

May your strength never falter
May you continue to lead with your kindness and love
May the burden you carry be less and less with each passing day
May you receive encouragement and blessings from *above*!

Special Needs

Angels

Some time back two angels were sent to care for a chosen girl or boy
Only the angels knew what they must do and what to say
They also knew where this chosen girl or boy lived
And stayed in that town each and every day

They followed this chosen boy or girl and guarded the child real close
The angels even helped dress the child and took the child to the grocery store
They helped feed the child and helped make the child's favorite meals
They pushed the child on the swing and never complained when the child asked for more

The angels also went and bought some real neat toys
And brought the toys to the child so that she or he could play
The angels were delighted to see the happy look on the child's face
But more importantly the angels saw how much love there was each and every day

The angels tried to help the child grow and do things on her/his own
But realized some tasks really caused the child lots of pain
The angels cried to see the child suffer, but never lost their faith
But the angels helped each other even more and vowed never to complain

The child grew with each passing year and the angels never left
The angels kept on doing what they must do to help the child grow
The angels kept on loving, caring, and supporting the child and made it clear,

"This is my child whom I will protect and defend"—that is what I
    want all to know

You see, when the angels were sent to help this special child,
Their mission was clear, and they did and will continue to complete
    the errand
The angels will stand firm and will forever show their strength and
    love
And you know what—these two angels are and will always be your
    parents

Rest assured, my child, that as your angel and parent I know what I
    must do
I will protect, defend, care, support, encourage, help, and will always,
    always love you

Choice

Do you think I had a choice?
I'll answer that and say no I did not have a choice
I did not wish or want to be what I am but
No one heard my cries no one heard my voice

But I am real and I am alive
I have feelings and just like you I have a heart
I may be different and many may not see me as they should
Some tend to avoid me and stand far apart

The cross that I bear is not contagious
The pain I feel or do not feel is real and true
The anguish I may feel when I am scorned is real
The looks I sometimes get makes me get sad and blue

Why do some people see me so different?
Why do some go out of their way to avoid me?
Why can't they understand that I did not have a choice?
Why is it that they have eyes but do not see?

I am alive and have a right to be here
I do have feelings even though I may not always show
My love, my tears, and sometimes hide my true being
But I am alive and that I do want all to know

Again, I did not have a choice on what I am
Nor do I know what I could have been if given a choice
Would I avoid those less fortunate than me or
Would I protest injustice and raise my voice?

One thought I do want to convey
Is that I was blessed beyond belief
And that thought is that I do have wonderful parents
Even though I may sometimes cause them sadness and grief

They did have a choice and they chose to be with and by me
And for that I will always look up to mom and dad
For their courage, strength and love without bounds
For their protection which makes me real glad.

Thanks mom and dad for making the right choice!
Even though I may not say it often—rest assured I love you!

Did You Notice?

Did you notice me applauding your child's accomplishments?
Did you by chance see the tear in my eye?
Did you notice the look of amazement I displayed?
Did you notice my body language, did you hear me sigh?

You see, I am so happy for you and your child
I notice that your child has been blessed beyond belief
I also captured the moment you looked so proud
But most of all I noticed how you finally relaxed, felt relieved

It must feel great to share in the success of your child
To master all kinds of challenges as they come
To excel in all your endeavors and exceed expectations
To be two persons in motion acting as one

I noticed your child does look up to you
For guidance, support, help, or motivation
I noticed how much love you display toward your child
I compliment you for your demeanor and inspiration

I applaud you and congratulate you and your child
I have no hatred, envy, jealousy, ill feelings toward anyone
I enjoy watching kids compete and show off their skill
And to me . . . bottom line is I do not care who lost or won.

But now let me tell you about me and my child
My child will never compete in organized sports
My child's accomplishments, with the grace of the Good Lord,
Will be many, but of a different sort.

The first word, first step, or sign of independence
Will be recorded and treasured in our mind and heart
I will feel so grateful, proud, honored and relaxed
I will be my child's mentor and coach . . . I'll play that part.

I'll guide, help, instruct, and teach my child
I'll teach about life and above all about love
I'll laugh and cry along the way but will never complain
I'll acknowledge effort made and pray for help from above

You see, in a way, we are not different
We both show our love and display our emotion
We both encourage, praise, and reward accomplishments
We both lead with love, patience, and devotion.

I look forward to see what tomorrow may bring
To see my child try to succeed . . . to see the motive
But above all, did you see the respect we have for each other?
The patience, guidance, inspiration, support and love . . .
I sure wish that was evident and that you did notice.

Guardian Angel

Hellllloooo! Hellllloooo!
Was the greeting directed at me.
I turned around and was amazed that the child
Greeting me was afflicted with muscular dystrophy

I also greeted this child and shook the child's hand
But in my mind, I thought—today an angel spoke to me
The child's parents were awestruck that this interaction took place
Again, I saw an angel not a person afflicted with muscular dystrophy

I even went so far to ask if this child was an angel
Child smiled and feverishly waved his/her hands
And I had to lean close to hear what the child said
And I heard—there are angels all over this land

When I go to therapy as I always do
I see a lot of angels gathered there
Angels taking care of my autistic or diabetic friends
Or my cancer friends that have lost their hair

Angels of all sicknesses taking care of each one of us
Taking care of all of us and our parents too
For our parents suffer lots, but never complain
Even though they suffer much more than we do

You see, there are angels everywhere
An angel has been assigned to each one of us
They take care of us at home or at play
At the therapist or on the school bus

The answer to your question—no I am not an angel
I am just a human being afflicted with muscular dystrophy
But one fact I do want you to know is that
Today, your guardian angel waved and greeted me!

Special Needs Parents

You see these loving parents everywhere
Cradling, pushing, or holding their child with pride
Always positive individuals displaying their patience
Encouraging their children to keep in stride

These are the special parents that we all have seen
Loving and protecting their child that needs their protection
Speaking lovingly, sweetly, and softly to their loved one
That may not understand or may not follow directions

Putting forth all efforts to take care of their loved one
Not being ashamed to take their loved one to the store
Buying and giving them candy, apples, bananas, or treats
Letting loved ones indulge when they ask for more

But even an outing can be a task
Not from the loved one but from others who can't understand
At how my loved one may act or look to them
But rest assured this is my loved one whom I will defend

We mean you no harm and we have a right to be here
For as you love and protect yours the same goes for us
We are here as a family and will try to bother no one
We will not create a ruckus or stir up a fuss

My only wish is that you would understand
I love my child no matter how he/she looks to you
I'll guide, help and care for their need
You need not judge us nor be in any way rude

If the tables were turned and I noticed your plight
I would try to be helpful and ask how I could be of assistance
Having been a special needs parent I would greet your loved one
And would try to interact with your child even though I was met
    with resistance

You see, we special needs parents do not ask for much
We want to be accepted as we are and for people to accept that truth
Approach us as humans, and we are not asking for pity
Just be a decent and caring human being and do not be rude

God chose us to be special parents for our special needs son/daughter
We accept the challenge to be a supportive/protective/caring/loving
    mother and father!

Strength

What would I give to be as strong as a person . . .
Pushing a loved one confined to a wheel chair for life
Staying positive and in control for a dying wife
Feeding a loved one who will never be capable of doing this
Not having anything in life but still full of bliss

Taking the time to help the elderly and one's left alone
Staying up all night, going to work and coming straight home
Helping a loved one living in pain and accepting realism
Caring for a child afflicted with autism

Pushing and grinding to make ends meet
Letting your child take all the glory . . . taking a back seat
Leading a loved one who can neither hear nor see
Pleading with the Good Lord . . . give me this sickness . . . give it to
     me

Pushing a wheel chair day in and day out
Terminally ill and on death bed but never shouts
Staying by loved one afflicted with Alzheimer until the end
These are true models—women or men

No glory or praise comes to these proud individuals that care for a
     sick/loved one
And even though I may not have covered all afflicted that I meant
I want you to know that I respect you, admire you and look up to
     you
And most of all I admire your determination, resilience, and strength!

May your strength never falter
May you continue to lead with your kindness and love
May the burden you carry be less and less with each passing day
May you receive encouragement and Blessings from *above*!

Kid's Stories

Anty

Many moons ago, there was an anthill that housed a colony of fire ants. There were many ants that lived within that anthill and colony. This particular ant colony was located real close to a church. This story is about one single ant that we will name Anty so that we can follow along with some of Anty's life experiences.

Anty's mom was named Goodie, and Anty's dad was named Jawsome. It's important to know Anty's mom and dad because they were bringing up Anty to be a strong and normal fire ant. Anty was already twice as big as some of the other fire ants that were his age, so Goodie and Jawsome knew their son was going to be special and would someday be a leader within the ant colony.

Anty was growing up to be a normal fire ant and was aware of all the fire ant rules within the colony, but Anty questioned some existing rules. Anty was a thinker and wanted to know why the colony did things that he thought they should not do. Anty was already developing leadership skills because he was not a follower but acted on some things on his own.

One of the rules Anty questioned was this rule:

1. If anyone steps on or destroys our anthill, we will attack intruder in numbers.

Anty thought that this was a ridiculous rule, and he wanted it changed to:

2. If anyone steps on or destroys our anthill on purpose to hurt ant colony, then we will attack intruder in numbers. Accidents should be forgiven and not attacked.

The current ant leaders paid Anty no mind and did not change their rule. One day, a poor unlucky dog stepped on the anthill. The poor dog was playing fetch with his owner and thought nothing of the anthill until the ants attacked. What the dog did not know or see was that Anty also raced out of the anthill and up the dog's leg, but Anty was trying to stop the other ants from biting the dog. Even though Anty was much bigger than most ants, he could not stop all the ants, so the poor dog was bitten. Anty felt sad that his brothers and sisters had acted so badly with the poor dog, but he knew he had not bitten the dog but tried his best to stop the others from biting.

Once Goodie and Jawsome heard what Anty had tried to do, they were mad and had a talk with Anty. They told Anty that he needed to follow the attack rule each and every time that their anthill was stepped on. Another point they made was that he needed to also bite the intruder. Anty told his parents he could not do that just because someone had made this silly rule. Kept arguing that accidents do happen and pointed out that the dog did not even know he had stepped on the anthill. Goodie and Jawsome just shook their head and told Anty that they would talk about this later.

By now, you have probably guessed that most of the ants did not like Anty, so most of the ants avoided being near or around him. Anty, not by choice, had become a loner ant within the colony, but his ideas never stopped, and he kept asking questions about all sorts of things.

Anty had plenty of time all by himself, and most evenings when most of the ants would go to sleep, Anty would go out of the anthill and just sit there and stare at the sky. He would bring his two front legs together and just sit there staring at the sky. Some of the other ants would ask, why is he outside and what is he doing? What is he looking at? Why does he do this every night? Most of the time, ants that were watching Anty would fall asleep, so they never knew if Anty stayed up all night or at what time he came back inside the anthill.

Anty was curious and wanted to know all about the stars, moon, clouds, and the heaven above. Anty wanted to know if anyone lived up there. Anty would just sit there every night and wonder what or who was up there and were they good or bad ants or people.

Anty was real curious, and when the other ants started talking about what Anty did every night, they decided to tell Goodie and Jawsome what their son did every night. One night, while Anty was sitting like he was praying, Goodie and Jawsome asked him what he was doing. Anty said he was looking for answers like who is up there and who is he?

Neither Goodie or Jawsome could answer Anty's question, so they left him and told him to be careful as he was outside the anthill by himself. Anty told them not to worry about him and that he knew how to take care of himself and needed to get answers to his questions.

One day, Anty decided to follow along behind a string of people that were going into this building, which was a church. No sooner had all gathered there when he heard a man in front tell all that today they would start the church service with the Lord's Prayer to praise God. Anty heard the group start and say, "Our Father who art in Heaven," and they kept saying the rest of the Lord's Prayer, but Anty had gotten his answer and did not listen to the rest of the prayer. He now knew that someone very important lived in the sky above because the prayer was called the Lord's Prayer, and they prayed to the Father who lives in heaven. They prayed to God.

Wow! Anty knew what he had to do every night, and tonight would be the beginning. Anty could not wait for night fall so that all the other ants would go to sleep and he could go outside and pray to the Father above. He had found his answer and purpose for his life.

Anty told the other ants about what he had learned and heard inside the building close by. He also said the Lord's Prayer in parts that he remembered such as Our Father who art in Heaven and forgive us our trespasses as we forgive those that trespass against us. Anty told them that this Lord's Prayer was just his rule, which was: if anyone steps on or destroys our anthill on purpose to hurt ant colony, then we will attack intruder in numbers. Accidents should be forgiven and not attacked.

We have to start forgiving those that trespass against us and not attack because that is what we are supposed to do. We have to forgive accidents and live peacefully just like all the people who were gathered inside the building next to our home.

Little by little, Anty's group started to grow as some of the others joined him at night in prayer and in trying to stop others from biting anyone that stepped on their home. Anty was making friends and never stopped trying to get more ants to think like he did. Anty was on a roll.

To this day, Anty is still trying to get all the ant colony—where he lives—to be just like him and his group of followers. If you go anywhere and see an anthill, look closely and see the biggest ant, you may just be looking at Anty. Keep in mind that Anty is still an ant and has never been touched by humans, so do not touch him or the other ants because if you do, they may bite thinking that you are trying to hurt them. Give Anty and his group room as they have lots of work to do to try and convince the other ants to live peacefully.

Moral of this story is that we can be different and question why we do some things, which we think are bad. We do not need to be bad because others are bad. We do not need to fight because others fight. We need to find God just like Anty wanted to know who lived up there in heaven and eventually found God. We need to learn to live in harmony and peace as the Lord said, "Peace I leave you; my peace I give you. I do not give to you as the world gives. Do not let your hearts be troubled, and do not be afraid."

Chopper, Chipper, and Cutter

Many moons ago, in a big lake, lived three particular beavers. Two of these beavers were brothers, and one was a friend. Let me introduce you to these three beavers so that we can follow some of their life experiences.

One of the beaver brothers was named Chopper, and the other beaver brother was named Chipper. Chopper was older than Chipper. Their friend was named Cutter and was as old as Chopper. Chipper was a lot stronger than Chopper and Cutter, and, sometimes, it was this strength not to mention his youth that got Chipper in trouble.

The three beavers lived in this very big lake with lots of water, but more importantly, they built their houses or beaver dams by a creek that flowed into the lake. They knew that running water could be controlled by their house or beaver dam. They would control amount of water that flowed from the creek into the lake. Blocking the water would allow the area behind their house or beaver dam to get flooded with water. This flooding also helped the beavers because the trees that they would cut were in the water or very close by. This helped the beavers as they are not very fast out of the water, and they were in danger if other bigger and meaner animals caught them too far away from water.

One day, Chopper told his younger brother to be careful as he went about his business of cutting trees next to his house or beaver dam. Chopper told Chipper that he was making too much noise as he swam in the water and also that he was cutting trees too far away from the water's edge. Chipper told Chopper that he could take care of himself and that he was just saying that because he was too old to do the same things that he, Chipper, could do.

Chopper just shook his head and knew well enough to let Chipper have the last word and not start an argument with his little brother. Cutter just listened, looked, and nodded his disapproval with what Chipper had told his older brother. Cutter wanted so badly to take up for his good friend Chopper, but knew he had better stay out of their conversation.

Chipper kept on being Chipper and kept on making all kinds of splashing noises while he swam, and because he was making all this noise to get Chopper mad, he failed to see the big black bear that was looking at him. Chipper was in serious trouble if he got too close to the bear. Luckily, for Chipper, his big brother, Chopper, and his friend, Cutter, started splashing the water with their tail real hard and loud to get Chipper's attention. This worked, and when Chipper looked at them, they told him to look behind him. When Chipper looked, he saw the big black and ugly bear looking at him. All three beavers made a dash for their house and beaver dams. Once inside, they were safe from the bear and anything else.

Chipper was glad that his brother and friend had warned him about the bear, but not glad enough to apologize to his big brother for the words he told him. Chipper still believed that his big brother, Chopper, was jealous because he was younger and stronger than he was.

Once the scare from the bear wore off, the three beavers came out of their house and beaver dam and scanned the shore for any signs of the bear or any other dangerous animal. Luckily, bear was gone, so it was back to work as they had to live up to their reputation, which was busy as a beaver.

Chopper and Cutter stayed close to the water, or in the water, as they chewed down some trees. Chipper, on the other hand, was still being Chipper, so he left the water and was chipping down trees too far away from the water line. He had totally ignored his big brother's advise and had placed himself in danger that he was not aware of.

Chopper was busy chipping down a tree, but he kept looking in the direction of Chipper to see if he was all right. Cutter kept doing the same, but he was really not too concerned about Chipper as he was about chipping down the tree he was working on.

As mentioned, Chopper, being older and much wiser than Chipper, knew about the dangers all beavers may face if they get caught by a bigger animal too far away from the water. No sooner had Chopper had this danger thought when he spotted a black object walking toward Chipper. Black object turned out to be the same black bear that they had seen earlier and was heading straight at Chipper.

Chipper was totally unaware of the approaching danger as he was making too much noise chipping away at a big tree he had chosen to knock down. Chopper knew he had to do something, but what? Chopper and Cutter started to make a lot of noise with their beaver tails as they had done earlier to warn Chipper of danger, but this time it did not work as Chipper was making too much noise and he was too far away.

Chopper was out of options, but he told Cutter to help him attack the bear so that Chipper could have time to get back into the water and his house or beaver dam. Cutter did not like that idea, and when Chopper started swimming toward the bear, Cutter started swimming to his house or beaver dam. Cutter thought that this would be the last time he would see Chopper. Chopper was on his own.

Chopper came out of the water at a dead run straight for the big black bear who was already close to Chipper. Bear was so close to Chipper that Chipper was now fully aware that bear was there, but he was also aware that there was no way he could get to the water before the bear caught him. Chipper was going to fight the bear or so he thought.

While Chipper was preparing to fight the bear, he noticed his brother, Chopper, passed him by and ran straight at the bear. This was Chipper's chance to get away, and he took off at a fast run toward the water. Chipper had no idea how his brother, Chopper, was doing with the big bear.

Chopper surprised the bear as these little beavers should run away from bigger and stronger bears, but not this beaver. What was his problem? Bear did not know that he was picking on his younger brother and that Chopper would defend at all costs. That is what brothers and family do for their loved ones, and Chopper was no exception.

The bear ran away from the crazy beaver that had reversed roles on him. The bear was supposed to scare the beaver, and not the other way around. This beaver was crazy, and the bear wanted no part of this, so off he ran into the woods.

Chopper returned to the water where Chipper was waiting and hugged and told his big brother that he was sorry for the unkind words that he had spoken earlier, and that, from now on, he would listen to his big brother's advise. Chopper hugged his little brother and told him he loved him and only wanted him to be safe and never ever get hurt. Chopper told Chipper he forgave him.

Cutter also came out of his house and approached Chopper and told him he was not a very good friend for not sticking close to him when he needed him to. Chopper told Cutter he understood and forgave him for not being by him as he attacked bear. Chopper told Cutter he was still his friend and would be his friend forever.

Next time you go by a lake or a pond and see three beavers swimming or working, you may just be looking at Chopper, Chipper, and Cutter. You may also see the brotherly love between Chopper and Chipper and notice the friendship bond they have with Cutter.

Moral of this story is that no matter how dangerous or serious the problem may be, God has given us a big brother to watch out and take care of us. In the Bible, it is written, "A friend loves at all times, and a brother is born for adversity" (Prov. 17:17).

Faith, Hope, and Love

Many moons ago, there was a man in our neighborhood that raised birds that could talk. The man we will call Mr. Birder just to follow his life's experience with these talking birds.

Mr. Birder had many birds that he raised to sell or to take to local festivals to show them to parents and kids at the festival. Birds were beautiful to look at and everyone laughed when they spoke like a human being. In particular, Mr. Birder had three very distinct and different birds that were Mr. Birder's favorites.

Different they were because there was a Scarlet Macaw parrot that was named Faith. Faith was beautiful to look at with her red and blue feathers. Faith was also the biggest of the three birds Mr. Birder really liked. Faith was the noisy one of the three, but she was really smart and would imitate anyone that spoke to her. Her only problem was that when she was not talking, she would constantly squawk real, real loud. The whole neighborhood could hear her squawking and often complained to Mr. Birder about the noise Faith made.

One of the other birds was an African Grey parrot that Mr. Birder named Hope. Hope has silver gray feathers but her tail feathers are bright red. Hope is about half the size of Faith, but is real pretty to look at. Hope is probably the smartest of the three favorite birds that Mr. Birder really liked. Hope liked to imitate people's voice, but she could also sing and whistle real loud. Mr. Birder also received some complaints when Hope would get in one of her "go through everything I know" attacks.

The last of the three favorite birds was a little green and blue parakeet that was named Love. Like I mentioned above, Love was a lot smaller than Faith and Hope. She could talk and whistle just like Faith and Hope, but she was not a loud one. Mr. Birder never received any complaints about Love. Her voice and whistles were not loud or annoying to anyone near or far off. Love was probably the most active of the three favorite birds as she was constantly jumping or flying from perch to perch within her cage.

All these birds lived in their own separate cage, but their cage was placed close enough to each other so that they could all learn what each one knew. They were a group to be around especially when they all started saying the same sentences or whistling the same song. It made people laugh and the more they laughed the crazier these three birds would act.

As mentioned, Mr. Birder really cared for these three favorite birds and would not sell them for any amount of money. They were his pets, and he treated them real good and fed them only the best birdseed, peanuts, and sunflower seeds on the market. The birds had a very good life and showed their appreciation to Mr. Birder by learning new words or songs as quickly as they could.

One morning, when Mr. Birder was cleaning out the cages of the other parrots or birds he had, the three favorite birds started a serious discussion. Faith, Hope, and Love had agreed to discuss which one of them was the greatest.

Faith, being the biggest and probably the meanest, said that she should go first to prove her point of why she was the greatest. Hope and Love agreed to let Faith go first just so Faith would not get offended. Faith said she was the greatest because the letter "F" in the alphabet comes before the letter H for hope and the letter L for love. Another point that Faith mentioned is that her name had one more letter than Hope and Love. She went on to say that, without Faith, you could not have hope or love. Both Hope and Love were amazed that Faith had spoken so well and really did a good job on why she should be the greatest.

Next up was Hope who started by saying that, without hope, you have nothing to hold on to. You cannot have faith or love without hope. Hope is what keeps one dreaming that things will get better and problems or sickness will go away. Hope also stressed that she always heard people say, "I hope you get better soon," or "I hope you can forgive me," or this one, "I hope tomorrow is better than today."

Hope is something that people always want, so I believe I am the greatest and without hope there is no faith or love. Wow! Hope had made her case real clear, and she made sense on why she should be the greatest of the three.

Next and the last one to prove why she should be the greatest of the three was Love. This was going to be hard to prove, but Love had a perfect plan that could not fail. Love started by speaking real good about why people need faith as real faith is a necessity that people must have. Love said that when people have really true faith that they also get love to go along with faith. She said just look at all people that have faith, and you will see that their faith leads them to love their parents, neighbor, and God. Wow! Love was on a roll.

Next point Love made was to speak very nice about hope. Love agreed with Hope and said that all people should have hope and never, ever lose hope. Love went on to say without hope, there is no tomorrow or any good things to come. People need hope so that their hope and faith allows them to be nice to other people or strangers that they meet for the first time. Love also stressed that where there is hope, there is love; and where there is hope, faith, and love, there is peace and there amongst all three there is God.

Love ended her case on why she should be the greatest, and I believe that Faith and Hope realized that Love had truly presented her case very well and that she was the greatest of the three, but before they said that Love was the greatest, Faith and Hope wanted to ask Mr. Birder who he thought was the greatest of Faith, Hope, and Love.

Once Mr. Birder was asked who the greatest of these three (Faith, Hope, and Love), he went into his house and came out with a book. He spoke to the birds and told them he had his Bible and would read what the Bible says about which one is the greatest between Faith, Hope, and Love. The three birds agreed that whatever was written in this book or the Bible would be the final on their discussion.

Do you know which one of the three—Faith, Hope and Love— is the greatest?

Mr. Birder read this passage from the Bible . . . "But now faith, hope, and love, abide these three; but the greatest of these is love."

The birds had gotten their answer, and it was written in the Bible that love is the greatest, but true to spirit, the parakeet named Love told Faith and Hope that her love would always be there because of Faith and of Hope.

Next time you hear a squawking parrot, you may have just heard Faith. If you are really lucky, you may see Faith, Hope, and Love. They would love to speak and sing for you.

Moral of this story is that we must always cling to our faith no matter what, and we must hold on very tight to hope and never let faith or hope go, but the most important thing we must always have is love for one another, and for our God who takes care of all of us!

Fluffy

Many moons ago, in a pasture close by, lived a young ram. We will name this young ram Fluffy so that we can follow Fluffy's life experiences.

Fluffy was a normal kid growing up. Fluffy would run and jump all throughout the meadow and up and down the mountainside. Fluffy was also very normal in so far that he did not always listen to his dad or mom. Fluffy did not have to listen as he thought he was not afraid of anything.

Fluffy's dad was named Hard Head because he could butt heads with other rams and always made the other rams back down. Fluffy's mom was named Lady E, and just like any normal and caring mom, she guarded Fluffy as best she could. Unfortunately, Fluffy was much younger, faster, and could go on and on without stopping to rest, and those traits made it real hard for Lady E to keep a close eye on him, but she was never too far from him.

One day, Fluffy was told by Hard Head and Lady E to stay close as they were in a different pasture and they did not know what dangers lurked in this new pasture. Fluffy, being a normal and inquisitive kid, decided that he did not have to heed his parents' advise and ventured off to explore on his own.

No sooner had Fluffy topped a rolling hill that blocked his view to his parents that Fluffy encountered his first lesson. Fluffy was going to eat some grass and, in particular, one flower, but when he bit into the flower, an agitated bee flew off the flower and stung Fluffy on his nose. The pain caused Fluffy to cry out in pain and started jumping up and down in the pasture.

When Hard Head heard Fluffy's cry, he ran over the hilltop and was ready to defend and confront any danger that was threatening Fluffy. Fortunately, the bee was long gone as this may have been a fight that Hard Head might have lost. Lady E arrived after Hard Head, scolded Fluffy, and told him to stay close to them. What do you think Fluffy would do?

You are correct, Fluffy went off again on his young adventure, and this time, he was startled when a butterfly landed on his nose. Fluffy remembered vividly the bee sting and let out a holler and started jumping and bucking again. This brought Hard Head at a dead run to his aid, but this time, he saw the culprit or the butterfly that was still trying to land on Fluffy's nose. Hard Head laughed so hard and told Fluffy that butterflies do not bite or hurt you.

Hard Head also told Fluffy that he needed to stay close and quit going off by himself as dangers were everywhere. Again, words of wisdom to an adventurous kid. What do you think Fluffy did? You are correct, he walked off again to do some more lone exploring.

Fluffy's trip took him near some wooded patches, and as he was walking, he happened to see a wolf that was staring right at him. Fluffy's instincts told him to run as fast as he could back to his dad and mom. Fluffy did just that. He started running and crying out real loud so that his dad, Hard Head, would hear and come to his rescue. Fluffy was running as fast as he could, but a backward glance revealed that the wolf was closing in on him. Fluffy was scared beyond belief.

Fluffy kept running and crying out for help and headed in the direction of his dad. Fluffy was getting tired and was slowing down, which helped the wolf come closer to him. Fluffy started thinking that he was going to be a meal for this bad wolf and was upset that he had not paid attention to his mom and dad. If he had paid attention, all this would not be happening.

Fluffy was about to stop and confront the wolf as he was so tired that he could not run anymore, but just prior to stopping, he saw Hard Head running as fast as he could right at Fluffy and the wolf. The wolf never saw what slammed into him, but the wolf saw and felt that he was no match for this angry dad, so he ran away from Fluffy and Hard Head.

Fluffy had survived a very bad lesson in life, but he also had learned that his father will do anything for him to keep him safe.

He learned this lesson well, and from that point on, Fluffy always listened to his dad no matter if his instincts told him differently.

Another learning point is that Hard Head always forgave his son for not listening, and once a learning experience passed, Hard Head never used that learning experience against Fluffy. Hard Head would ram heads and confront any danger for his son, but he was also very caring and loving toward his son.

If you are lucky, next time you go by a pasture and if you see a young ram running and bucking in the pasture, you have seen Fluffy at his very best. Look some more and you will see Hard Head nearby protecting his son.

Moral of this story is that we humans/Christians do not always listen when our Father speaks to us, but just like Hard Head, our Heavenly Father is always there to protect, defend, and love us no matter what obstacles we might be facing. We, just like Fluffy, tend to stray and go on some good and bad adventures, but our God always welcomes us back, forgives us, and is always there to protect us. Believe in the Father and the Son!

Harmony

Many moons ago, there lived a humming bird who, for the purpose of this story, we will name Whirly. In the same area, there was a honey bee who we will name Buzzer. Now, Buzzer and Whirly shared their area with a butterfly who was named Lady Flutter. Whirly, Buzzer, and Lady Flutter knew each other quite well.

It was always enjoyable to sit outside and watch the beauty of the garden. There were rose bushes with beautiful and sweet smelling roses, gardenia plants with white flowers that smelled divine, basil with aroma filling your nose with an unforgettable, and pleasant aroma and hibiscus plants with beautiful flowers, which were red, orange, and yellow.

All these plants had flowers that attracted Whirly, Buzzer, and Lady Flutter on a daily basis. It was a guarantee that Whirly, Buzzer, and Lady Flutter would visit the garden at least once each and every day.

What I found fascinating was that Whirly, Buzzer, or Lady Flutter never seemed to fight if the flower they were to pull some of the nectar juice out of was already occupied. There were plenty of flowers in the garden and plenty of time during the day to come back to this one flower. There was harmony in the garden.

I recollect one instance where all three—Whirly, Buzzer, and Lady Flutter—landed at exactly the same time on the same flower. I looked to see what was going to happen and was surprised that all three stared at each other as they hovered above the flower they all had visited. Seemed like they just eyed each other as each one of their wings moved to keep them above the flower. I believed that they were talking to each other as, all of sudden, Whirly flew off to another flower as did Buzzer who also left and landed a few feet away on a different flower. I guess the two gentlemen decided that they would leave and let Lady Flutter have the flower they all desired.

Once Lady Flutter had gotten her fill of nectar juice from the flower, she flew off to another flower to resume feeding. Once Lady Flutter left, it was evident that Buzzer was next as Whirly left one flower and went to another. Logically, when Buzzer left, here came Whirly, and he drank whatever nectar juice was left inside the flower.

I wished I had filmed this episode because it is even hard for me to believe, and yet, I witnessed this occurrence. There was peaceful harmony from three very different and distinct insects and bird.

So when you have some free time, go out onto your home garden or visit a plant nursery and if you are lucky, you will see Whirly, Buzzer, or Lady Flutter drinking sweet nectar juice from a sweet smelling and beautiful flower.

Moral of this story is that if Whirly, Buzzer, and Lady Flutter, who are totally different from one another, can live in peaceful harmony alongside each other, then we—as humans—should also do the same. God created the birds, bees, butterflies, and beautiful flowers because they were pleasant to look at and for our enjoyment so that we could live in peace and harmony with each other no matter what our differences are. Mother Nature has taught her students well as evident by how well Whirly, Buzzer, and Lady Flutter got along. Now is the time for all humans to live in peaceful harmony no matter what our differences may be.

God loves us the way we were created and does not abandon us because we are different!

Honker

Many moons ago there was a team of geese that lived in Canada. There were twenty-six geese that made up this team of geese. This team of geese was led by a male goose named Glyder. Glyder's mate was named Hydee, and their young son or goose was named Honker. Let's follow along on some of the life experiences that Glyder, Hydee, and Honker had.

Glyder, because he was the team leader, would tell the rest of the team when it was time to leave their home in Canada due to the cold weather. It was hard for geese to eat when the ground was full of snow or ice. So, every winter, when the weather turned real cold, this team led by Glyder would fly south to Texas and warm weather. It was not hard to find food in South Texas no matter if it was cold because, in South Texas, it hardly snowed.

One cold day, Glyder told his team that tomorrow, they would start their flight to South Texas. Glyder told all his team to get plenty of rest tonight because the trip would be hard and too long. Glyder also told the team to eat as much as they could today because they would need the energy and strength to fly many, many hours.

The news Glyder told the team made Honker real happy because he had not been on this trip before and was really looking forward to this trip. Honker did not listen and did not eat all he could have or get the necessary rest because he was so excited to be making his first trip to South Texas.

In the morning, Glyder gave his usual command to his team that he was ready to start the flight trip. Glyder would raise his neck as high as he could, wave his wings back and forth, and let out three distinct goose calls. This was the signal that he was ready and that the team needed to follow.

After his command, Glyder ran on the ground alongside other team members until they had enough speed to go up in the air and fly. Honker and Hydee were not far behind Glyder. All the team members were finally in the air and Glyder, being the team leader, made sure all his team was following.

Once all the team was in the air, they formed or flew in the form of the letter "V." Glyder being the leader was the one that was at the front of all the other geese. Honker and Hydee were the second and third goose behind Glyder. Geese fly in this formation to help each other fly farther without getting tired. The one in front, which was Glyder, was breaking the wind for the other geese, so the rest of the team did not have to move their wings too fast to break the wind. Glyder was doing all the work for now.

Soon, Glyder started to get tired, so he motioned to Honker to take over the lead or the point. Honker, being young, strong, and not knowing any better, was ready to accept the lead. He flew in front of Glyder and took the lead. Once Honker was in the lead, Glyder fell back to the end of the formation so that he could rest.

Honker was so excited to be in the lead that he was not pacing himself but was flapping his wings too fast. Hydee, his mom, told him to slow down or he would not last as the lead for very long. Honker heard his mom, but decided not to listen and kept flying at a very fast pace.

Glyder realized that the team was complaining because Honker was pushing them too hard and fast, so he flew up to Honker and told him the same thing Hydee, his mom, had told him. Honker again did not listen because he was so excited to be a leader on his very first trip.

Glyder flew to the back again to rest some more, but he kept a close eye on the team's progress and knew that soon, they would land somewhere to eat and rest for the night before beginning the trip again tomorrow. Glyder gave the signal with a loud goose call, and all the geese started flying downward to land in a pasture. Once all the geese landed, they were allowed to find food and eat, and all were told that the trip would begin very early in the morning.

Glyder had some advise for his son, Honker, but again Honker was still so excited that he never heard a word his father, Glyder, said.

Again, Honker did not eat or rest like he was told to. Honker was real excited that he was seeing land that he had never seen before. How could anyone eat or sleep when he was having so much fun?

It was the usual custom for geese to pray every night before going to sleep. All the team members would pray before going to sleep. The geese would fold their neck toward their wing and say a quick prayer. Glyder made sure all prayed before sleeping. Glyder also prayed, just like all the other geese, for strength and for direction so that they could endure the trip and not get lost. Once Glyder had finished praying and giving thanks for getting this far and for strength and direction, he would give out two loud calls, which signaled that praying time was over and now it was rest time.

As you probably know, Honker was still curious about this new land and was exploring and did not pray or go to sleep as he was supposed to. Honker had trouble listening to instructions.

Early in the morning, Glyder gave his three very distinct and loud goose calls to signal that it was time to start the trip. All the geese except, guess who, was not up and ready for the flight? You are right, Honker was still asleep even though no one but Honker could sleep through the calls Glyder made. Hydee pecked at Honker to wake up before his daddy got mad at him.

Honker was not too happy waking up so early. It seemed like he had just gone to bed, which he had. He had not gotten the rest he was supposed to. Hydee knew this, but did not tell Glyder because that would have upset him very much. Hydee knew Glyder would say, "How can he be a leader when he does not listen?"

Once the geese were in the air, Glyder took the lead as all leaders do. Hydee and Honker flew in their second and third place as was the normal thing to do, being that they were related to the leader. Once Glyder started to get tired, he motioned to his son, Honker, to take over. "Yea! I get to lead again," was Honker's reply. He was ready, or so he thought.

Honker did not fly very far before he started going off in the wrong direction. His speed was very slow compared to yesterday and compared to the pace the geese were used to. The team was having trouble staying in "V" formation because they were flying so slow.

Glyder noticed that Honker was falling asleep and not holding to the direction of travel that he should be taking. Glyder flew up to Honker to see if he was all right or if he was sick. Honker told his dad, Glyder, that he was not sick, but real tired and hungry.

Glyder had to stop the flight trip because of Honker. He gave out his usual stop flight call and all the geese started flying downward to land somewhere. Glyder was not too happy to stop the flight so soon especially since they were not even halfway to South Texas yet.

After the usual dad to son lecture about listening and about following directions or instructions, Glyder left Honker alone. Honker had learned his lesson and found food to eat, and boy did he eat, Honker even fell sound asleep before most of the team, but not before giving thanks and praying for strength and for direction. This time, Honker even prayed for patience for his dad and for obedience for him. He must start to listen to his parents who always want the best for their son or daughter. Honker was a changed goose. He had grown up a lot on this trip and knew he had to listen to keep him out of trouble.

The rest of the trip to South Texas was just a sightseeing adventure to Honker, and not once did he not listen to his parents or forget to pray. Honker now would make a very good team leader and his mom, Hydee, and his dad, Glyder, were extremely proud of him from this point on.

Who knows, next winter, when it is real cold outside and you hear a team of geese flying by, go outside and look at them. Look for the biggest and loudest goose, and you just may have seen Honker leading his team to a better place.

Moral of this story is twofold:

First is that we must all learn to listen to our parents' advice no matter if we are young or old, excited or not. Parents only want to help us grow up the right way and not get into any trouble whatsoever. Parents love us more than we will ever know.

Secondly is that we must always give thanks to our God for the direction He gives us, and also when we pray, we should always ask for strength and direction to make it through another day. Honk! Honk!

Lightning Bug

M any moons ago there was a certain lightning bug that did not know how to turn on his built in lamp. For all practical purposes we will name this lightning bug Burned Out so that you and I can follow Burned Out's journey through life.

Every day, at dusk, all the lightning bugs would go out of their hiding places to look for food or a mate. Burned Out was no exception as he mingled with all his friends and flew alongside them from place to place. Only exception was that Burned Out depended on others to light his way as he did not know how to turn on his built in lamp.

This inability to light his own way was very disappointing for Burned Out and to make matters worse all the other lightning bugs would make fun of him and call him ugly names and laugh at him. This caused Burned Out much sadness as he wanted to be part of the group and not the one they picked on constantly or on a daily basis. It got to the point where he did not want to go out every night alongside his friends.

Burned Out lived next to a school ground and he often wondered if others that were special experienced the same bullying that he encountered daily. He was so dejected that he was not eating properly, exercising, or going out with his so called friends.

One day Burned Out did get his answer… there on the school ground was a young boy that his so called friends picked on and made his life miserable as did my so called friends. Burned Out felt that this young boy was desperate for friendship, acceptance and love much like he. Burned Out knew he had to do something to help this young boy.

Once the young boy was left alone, Burned Out flew and landed on the boy's hand. The young boy was startled but sensed that this lightning bug meant him no harm. Little boy touched Burned Out and he did not bite or fly off. A friendship had been born.

Both Burned Out and the young boy were ecstatic about their new friendship and everywhere that the young boy went Burned Out was taken inside the boy's shirt pocket. Once the young boy would stop and sit he would reach into his pocket and gently pull out Burned Out. Boy would pet Burned Out and once told Burned Out that he was his best friend. This excited Burned Out and his internal lamp came on and it was the brightest lamp in the whole world. Burned Out was happy and he had learned how to turn on his built in lamp. Both friends were overjoyed at this occurrence.

Unfortunately, the boys at school kept picking on Burned Out's friend and this made Burned Out real sad. I do not know how this happened but a plan was devised. The young man would place Burned Out in his pocket and when the other kids would pick on him he would tell them he could do something they could not. He also told them that they had to be in a dark room for them to see his gift or power.

Like all normal kids they accepted out of curiosity and went into a dark room to see this power. Once all were inside the dark room the young boy touched his shirt pocket which was in front of his heart. This touch was a signal to Burned Out to unleash his power. Burned Out went out of his way and lit the boy's area in front of his heart that all that were gathered there were amazed. All were amazed that he could light up his heart just by touching it. Wow!

This occurrence helped the young boy's acceptance by the other kids but more importantly they stopped picking on the young boy. This made Burned Out and the young boy very, very happy. To this day Burned Out and the young boy, even though both have grown up, remain best of friends.

If you have seen a lightning bug, you have probably seen Burned Out as he has the brightest built in lamp and lights up the darkness to show his happiness at being accepted, respected by friends, and more importantly loved by his friends and by his best human friend.

You see, God works in mysterious ways to help all—human or bug—enjoy life. We just have to be observant and look for His light. He will show and light our way out or from our troubles, worries, or fears!

Magical Book

My little girl came up to me and out of the blue asked
Daddy, what's it like to get old?
I knelt down and looked at her deep blue eyes
Knowing full well I had lost control

You see, a little girl that's just past five
Should not think that 30 is way too old
But how do you answer such a simple question
Without showing that somehow you've lost control

I said I'd try to explain where she would understand
Not understanding that at 30 I was showing my age
I said life is like a magical book with lots of surprises
And every smile, tear, bad, or good thing is in each magical book page

There is even a page when you were born
And even how happy and proud you made your mother and me
Each page is filled with what we say and do and how we treat others
In fact, it's pretty good at naming all in our family tree

But back to explaining how it feels to get old
Your Magical Book only has five pages all told
But my Magical Book has many, many more pages
Which is part of the benefit of getting old

You see, each page tells a story of me and my life
It tells of how I went from being your age to being your dad
Getting old is leaving your friends and childhood behind
Not letting the things that bothered you get you mad

Getting old is loving family a heck of a lot more
Treating others with the very utmost respect
Getting a job to buy you food and toys and more
Making a vow, "family—never neglect"

My Magical Book also tells of the many aches and pains I have
About gaining some weight and about my hair loss
It also tells of how I worry and care for you and mom
Says it's only normal to worry about you two without a cause

You see, getting old is not too—too bad
Why? It only increases the pages in your Magical Book
And you know what? You are in control of what is on each page
It can show you smiling and beautiful or angry with a hateful look

Have I truly answered your question on what's it like to get old?
Did I take the time to explain and did you understand?
Again, our own Magical Book tells a lot about each one of us
Being a little girl, little boy, woman, or man.

The choice is yours on how you want your Book to read
You decide the path and how you treat others in your life
You decide if you want to be good or bad or simply do not care
You'll even decide on whether you will be a good mother and wife

Your mom and I hope we have shown you the right path
As it will all be written in your Magical Book
We know that when we read your pages out loud to each other
We both will shed a tear or two while proudly reading the good path
     you took!

P.S. It took a child that was barely five
To ask a question, how does it feel to get old?
Maybe I'll ask my dad and see if it surprises him
And like me—causes him to lose control!

Miracle

Many moons ago, there was a family that lived in a big city. This family was considered to be special due to their names. Let me introduce you to this family so that we can follow some of their life experiences.

The dad was named Harman E. Giver, the mom was Love Giver, and the small daughter was Miracle Giver. Due to their first name, and of course their last name, was why most thought this family was special.

Now, Miracle was about to turn four years in a couple of months, so she was not yet in any school classroom. Miracle though was a thinker, and like every little girl loved to play on the playground or playhouse with her dolls and toy dishes. Miracle was very active, and sometimes her mother, Love, had to tell Miracle to slow down or she might get hurt. Love and Miracle were real close to each other and loved each other dearly. Miracle talked to her mother much more than to her father because most of the time, daddy was at work.

One day, when Miracle was playing with her dolls and watching TV, a commercial for the Children's Hospital was aired on TV. Miracle was all attention especially when she noticed some of the kids at the hospital were her age, younger or older, but all were good-looking boys and girls. Hospital was asking for money donations to care for the medical needs of these children. Miracle knew she had to help after she watched this TV commercial.

Miracle started to think on how she could help but did not know how, yet. She decided to speak to mom as moms know everything. Unfortunately, it was Sunday morning when Miracle decided to ask, Love, her mom, about what she could do; but when she approached mom, Miracle was told to hurry and get dressed as they had to go to church. Love told her daughter that they could talk after church mass.

Once they were in church, the priest started talking about God and what He says through the Bible. Priest went on to say that Jesus performed many miracles and still does today. Went on to say that Jesus would heal all that came to him and spoke about the mustard seed and about having enough faith that nothing is impossible for you. Priest went on to talk about the woman that was sick and bleeding, and when she touched Jesus's clothes, she was healed. Jesus told the woman that her faith had healed her.

Everyone knows that God works in mysterious ways, and here was this almost four-year-old paying attention to the sermon at church. Not only was she paying attention, but it seemed like God was speaking only to her and gave her the answer to how she could help the kids at the Children's Hospital.

Once church mass was over and after the customary trip to a local restaurant to have breakfast, Harmon E., Love, and Miracle were back home. Miracle rushed to her room to change out of her Sunday church clothes. Then rushed back down to talk to her mom, Love, about what she planned to do.

Unfortunately, Harmon E., her dad, had other plans for her. He was taking us to a baseball game and then ride out to the country just to see the sites. My talk with mom was put on hold until tomorrow when dad left for work. Dad told us to get ready, and as soon as we were ready to go, to come outside where he would be waiting. Dad said he was going to water his very pretty rose bushes, hibiscus, and gardenia plants plus all the other plants that had beautiful flowers. Dad was very proud of his flower garden.

Miracle did not enjoy the game or the trip to the country as she was still thinking of her plan to help the kids at the Children's Hospital. She was truly excited when they arrived back home and that it was almost time to go to bed. She knew she would have trouble sleeping as she wanted to tell her mom about her plan and see what mom would think of her plan.

Finally, the minute arrived that dad left for work, so Miracle asked her mom if they could talk as she had promised they would do today. Mom said, "Okay, let's talk, and let's see what's up your sleeve." Miracle started by telling mom about the TV commercial for the Children's Hospital, and that they needed money donations to help take care of the children in the hospital. Mom was all ears and wondered what plan Miracle had to help.

Miracle gave mom her answer. Miracle said that in dad's flower garden, there are many beautiful flowers, and in the garage, there are many glass jars—big and small. Miracle went on to say that she could cut some of these flowers and sell them for a quarter. She also went on to say that she would not charge for the jar or the water the flower was in. Miracle also said that she would label the flowers, "Faith Flowers." Said that at church, the priest had said that Jesus said that if you have faith, the size of a mustard seed that nothing is impossible or if you truly believe that you will be healed, then your faith has healed you.

Love knew that her daughter had made a very strong argument on why she should allow the cutting of flowers from her dad's garden and decided to give her the approval to carry on with her plan. Mom, Love, asked her daughter how she could help, and Miracle told her that she did not know how to put up signs to show she was selling Faith Flowers for a quarter. Love said she could take care of the stand to place the jars on and of making the signs to advertise the selling of her Faith Flowers. Mom also created a sheet to show Miracle how much money she should get when she sells her Faith Flowers for a quarter. On the sheet, mom showed what one-quarter looks like, she also showed that five nickels or two dimes and one nickel make up a quarter. Mom told Miracle that there are more ways that she could get paid to equal one quarter, but she said that if she, Miracle, needed help that she would be inside the house and would be more than willing to help for this wonderful thing that she was doing.

It wasn't long after Miracle placed her first jars with water and one very pretty flower in each jar that people walking by and people driving by would read her sign and stop. Most wanted to ask why are those Faith Flowers, and when Miracle explained to them that if they believed in Jesus and in this flower, they could be healed, but more importantly that the money she would get from selling these flowers would be given to the local Children's Hospital so that kids in the hospital can have faith and money and be healed.

Who can pass up on a salesperson like that? Miracle was selling Faith Flowers as quickly as she could put them on sale, plus she still was not charging for glass jars, which made mom real glad to get rid of those jars.

Every story has a bad turn somewhere and this was no exception. When Harmon E., also known as dad, came home and saw that most of his pretty flowers had been cut, he threw a fit. His anger was aimed at Miracle when he saw the glass jars with his pretty flowers inside. He was furious and let Miracle know he was mad. So mad that he grounded her and told her she was not allowed to play with her dolls or watch TV for one week. Miracle only nodded and did not say anything, but went up to her room to cry.

When Love heard what Harmon E., her supposed to be caring husband, had done to Miracle, she was mad to the point that she approached Harmon E and told him what his daughter was doing and what the purpose was for selling the flowers. Harmon E. felt real sad that he had reacted the way he had and shed some tears in front of his wife. Harmon E. was truly hurt and wanted so much to tell his daughter that he was truly sorry and that she should continue selling flowers to help kids in the hospital. Harmon E. was so sad about what he had done. He even told Miracle he was sorry and that tomorrow, he would go buy her some more plants with flowers so that she could continue selling her Faith Flowers. Again, God was working in His own mysterious ways.

Miracle had sold many flowers and gotten rid of many glass jars that they had plus others that the neighbors donated. Miracle was truly a very good business young girl, and she had planned very well to get needed money for the Children's Hospital, and more importantly for kids that looked like her.

The day finally arrived—dad, Harmon E., mom, Love, and the young salesgirl named Miracle would go over to the hospital and donate all the money Miracle had made on selling her Faith Flowers. Once at the hospital, they were escorted to the office of the director, and once there, Miracle told her the reason that she had collected this money and said that she hoped that this money would help some of the kids if not all get better and that they would be able to go home.

The director's eyes, along with Miracle's parents' eyes, filled up with tears. They all knew this little girl was special and rightly named.

Miracle presented $1500 dollars to the director, and told her that she did not know if this was a lot or if it was not very much, but that she had sold plenty of flowers that her daddy had in the garden plus all the other flowers daddy had bought for her.

The director was speechless and asked Miracle and her parents if they wanted to see some of the kids in the hospital. Miracle jumped up with joy and excitement like never seen before, and she hollered, "Yes!" Miracle visited many a young boy and girl that were in the hospital and told them all that she had brought money so that they could have needed medicine and care. There was joy and excitement, not only in Miracle's eyes, but in the eyes of all the sick kids that she was allowed to visit. That day, Miracle gave ten kids she visited a Faith Flower.

Who knows, next time a visitor comes to the Children's Hospital with a donation, you may just be looking at Miracle.

Moral of this story is that God does work in mysterious ways, but *He* still performs miracles if you have faith the size of a mustard seed or truly have a lot of faith in God and Jesus, which will allow *his* love to come to you, allow you to live in harmony, and ultimately allow *him* to work *his* miracle. Thank God for Love, Harmon E., and Miracle, and let's all hope that we can learn and mimic their beautiful Christian way. Let's be like the Givers and give some of our time or money to help those truly in need. God Bless!

Mousetie

M any moons ago, a mouse lived inside the house of Mrs. Doogood. Mr. Doogood had gone up to heaven some years back and that is why the house belonged only to Mrs. Doogood and of course the mouse, or so she thought.

This mouse, for the sake of this story, we will name Mousetie so that we can follow some of Mousetie's life experiences. Mrs. Doogood's house is down the street from where you and your parents live. Mousetie is practically your neighbor.

Mrs. Doogood had retired some years back and had planned well for her retirement. When she was working, she made lots of money and used the money she made very well. Mrs. Doogood liked jewelry, and she liked the really expensive jewelry, so she shopped where she could get real nice and expensive jewelry. Mrs. Doogood had and always bought some really nice and expensive rings, bracelets, watches, earrings, and necklaces. Her jewelry was worth a lot of money, but because she lived alone, she left all her jewelry on top of one of her dresser chests.

Here is where Mousetie comes in. Mousetie had chosen her home very well as she also liked the shiny gold, silver, stainless, nickel, and titanium metals that was used to make the jewelry Mrs. Doogood had. Mousetie loved this jewelry so much that little by little, she would borrow some of Mrs. Doogood's jewelry and take it to her house, which was located behind one of Mrs. Doogood's stands. This stand was located in Mrs. Doogood's living room, which was close to the kitchen where Mousetie would get her late night snacks. Mousetie had again chosen her homesite very well.

Little by little, Mousetie was borrowing Mrs. Doogood's jewelry and taking it to her place of hiding. Mousetie loved to look at the very shiny jewelry and would oftentimes fall asleep on top of the jewelry that she had borrowed. Mousetie was a very typical female that liked jewelry.

One day, Mrs. Doogood was looking for some earrings that she knew she had, but could not find them. She looked and looked and never found these particular earrings. Mrs. Doogood had to settle on another pair to wear. She had plenty of earrings, so she was not concerned when she did not find this certain pair of earrings.

Mrs. Doogood had forgotten about the lost pair of earrings, but on another occasion, she was looking for a certain ring, which she had but could not find. She looked and looked and finally gave up when she could not find this ring and settled for another ring she had. She had many rings, and again, she was not concerned when she did not find this certain ring.

Mousetie, in the mean time, was enjoying looking and touching the earrings and rings that Mrs. Doogood was looking for. She was also loving all the other jewelry she had borrowed from Mrs. Doogood. Mousetie would occasionally place her arm through the rings she had borrowed and say, "Perfect fit," even though she could put all her legs inside ring, and still the ring would be too big for her. Mousetie did not care that rings were too big.

Mrs. Doogood wanted to wear a beautiful gold bracelet that Mr. Doogood had given to her on her fiftieth birthday, but again, she could not find this bracelet. Mrs. Doogood had to settle for another bracelet, but now she was concerned because this bracelet had been a gift from her husband whom she loved very much.

Mrs. Doogood suspected that someone was taking her jewelry, but who could it be? She did not let anyone go in to her bedroom, not even her grandchildren or daughters. Mrs. Doogood always kept her bedroom door locked to protect all her expensive jewelry. Mrs. Doogood knew she had to do something, but what could she do?

Mrs. Doogood called the police and asked that a detective come over, investigate, and see if the detective could find who was taking her expensive jewelry. The police detective that was sent to Mrs. Doogood's house started her investigation after Mrs. Doogood filled her in on all the jewelry that she was missing. Detective was shown what jewelry was left and where she stored all her jewelry.

Police detective looked and looked for clues to see if she could find who was taking Mrs. Doogood's jewelry, but could not find any clues at all. The jewelry had mysteriously disappeared. If the detective asked you if you knew anything what would you tell her?

After speaking to Mrs. Doogood, the detective and Mrs. Doogood agreed to set up cameras aimed at the jewelry. This way, if any more jewelry was taken, they would be able to see the person taking the jewelry and get Mrs. Doogood's jewelry back, or so they thought.

Mousetie knew nothing about the installation of cameras as she would not come out of her home when humans were moving about. She did not know that next time that she borrowed Mrs. Doogood's jewelry that she would be on camera, and the mystery of who is taking jewelry would be solved.

Sure enough, Mousetie was up to her old tricks of borrowing, and she decided to borrow another ring from Mrs. Doogood. Mousetie was caught borrowing once the camera tape was looked at, and it was not long before the police detective and Mrs. Doogood saw Mousetie grabbing and sneaking off with Mrs. Doogood's ring.

A plan was set in place by the detective and Mrs. Doogood—mouse traps with cheese, peanut butter, and crackers were set all over the house to catch Mousetie. Mousetie was on borrowed time and had to be real careful not to get caught. Mousetie could smell all the good treats that were set out for her to eat, but avoided these for the present time, but it was getting harder and harder to pass them up and look for food elsewhere.

One evening, when Mrs. Doogood had gone to sleep, Mousetie noticed a strange and awful smell. Mousetie came out of her house and noticed that a cooking pan was on fire and ran to the stove to see if she could turn out the fire. The fire was getting bigger inside the pan, and the smell was getting a lot worse. What could she do was what Mousetie was thinking.

Mousetie ran to Mrs. Doogood's bedroom and jumped up on the bed and started jumping on Mrs. Doogood's chest so that she would wake up. It worked, but when Mrs. Doogood woke up, she screamed and knocked Mousetie off the bed. Mousetie ran straight for the kitchen and Mrs. Doogood was right behind her. Mousetie stopped in front of the stove, and that is when Mrs. Doogood noticed that a pan was on fire. Mrs. Doogood turned off the fire and realized that Mousetie had saved her life. This point was proven when the detective and Mrs. Doogood looked at the camera film and saw Mousetie jumping up and down her chest to wake her up. Mousetie meant her no harm, but only wanted to warn her of danger in the kitchen.

The next morning, Mrs. Doogood picked up all the mousetraps they had set and threw them in the trash can. Mousetie was now her friend and roommate. To prove that she was pleased with Mousetie, Mrs. Doogood would place cheese and crackers or other goodies on a plate in the kitchen for Mousetie to eat. Mousetie was in mouse heaven!

Mrs. Doogood went so far as to go buy Mousetie some fake and shiny jewelry at a local department store. Mrs. Doogood now knew Mousetie loved jewelry just like she did, so she set this inexpensive jewelry next to Mousetie's plate of food. Wow! Mousetie was really in mouse heaven as she was getting food and jewelry, which were the two best things in the world for her.

Mousetie would take the fake jewelry, but in return Mousetie would trade the fine expensive jewelry that she had borrowed from Mrs. Doogood. Mrs. Doogood eventually had her rings plus all her other jewelry that she was missing plus the bracelet that her husband had given to her on her fiftieth birthday. Mousetie, on the other hand, well, she was still in mouse heaven because now she had her own jewelry, which was bought for her and which was not borrowed. She was truly in mouse heaven! Mousetie loved Mrs. Doogood, and she loved Mousetie.

Who knows, next time you see a mouse in your house, you may just be looking at Mousetie. Be sure to let your parents know so that Mousetie can be caught and released outside so that she can go home to where she belongs and that is with Mrs. Doogood.

Moral of this story is that God works in mysterious ways. God sends angels to us in the form of a mouse, cat, dog, hamster, rabbit, or in the form of parents. God is always protecting us and keeping us safe by sending his angels to warn us of any danger. So next time your parents tell you to do something or to stop doing something, it may just be that God sent this angel to warn you of danger. Listen to your parents at all times.

Purr-Fect

M any moons ago, there lived a grandma with her very pretty Siamese cat. We will name Grandma, Joyful, and her Siamese cat, we will name Purr-Fect so that we can follow some of their life's lessons. Now, Joyful and Purr-Fect live down the street from your house and my house.

Grandma Joyful cared and loved her pet cat, Purr-Fect, so much that she did not think Purr-Fect was a cat, but was her child. Grandma Joyful took real good care of Purr-Fect. Grandma let Purr-Fect do whatever he wanted to do inside the house. Grandma did not mind if Purr-Fect broke a lamp or ruined the window cords or even if he slept on top of the kitchen table. This house belonged to Purr-Fect as much as it did to Grandma Joyful.

I truly believe that Purr-Fect knew that he could do anything and get away with it because Grandma Joyful loved him dearly. Grandma Joyful would get up every morning with Purr-Fect right beside her in bed. Both Grandma Joyful and Purr-Fect felt real comfortable and safe while sleeping next to each other. Both took care of one another as best they could.

Every morning, Purr-Fect would follow Grandma Joyful when she got out of her bed. Grandma Joyful would go straight to the kitchen pantry and fill up Purr-Fect's bowl with some very good food. It was always a mystery what Purr-Fect would be fed, but Purr-Fect knew that Grandma Joyful cared and loved him so much that he would get fed before she even had her first cup of coffee, much less her breakfast. This day, Purr-Fect was fed some fish cereal that was delicious. Purr-Fect was in heaven eating this delicious breakfast meal.

Grandma Joyful always watched Purr-Fect eat his meals just to be sure that he ate good and to be sure he liked what she had bought for him. Grandma Joyful, according to Purr- Fect, really knew how to buy his food as he liked everything that she gave him.

After every meal, Purr-Fect would show his love to Grandma Joyful by rubbing his body on her legs and purring softly all the while. This constant back and forth rubbing and soft purring pleased Grandma Joyful a lot. It seemed to show that Purr-Fect was very happy, and if he was happy, so would she be. There was true harmony between Grandma Joyful and Purr- Fect.

Once Grandma Joyful sensed that Purr-Fect was getting tired of rubbing and purring, she would tell him to go outside, play for a while, and do other things cats may do outside the house. Grandma would let him out and always cautioned him to be careful and not to jump the fence into the alley or neighbor's yard. Sometimes, just to be sure Purr-Fect did not leave their yard, she would sit outside and watch him run around and play.

Purr-Fect enjoyed his time outside the house as there were plenty of things to do. He had to show Grandma Joyful his love and appreciation by keeping her yard clear of any bugs, lizards, snakes, or toads. Purr-Fect did not want any of these creatures to scare Grandma Joyful, so every time he was outside, he looked for these animals and ran them away from their yard. Purr-Fect tried to take care of Grandma Joyful just as good as she took care of him. Purr-Fect loved Grandma Joyful a lot, and he felt her love every minute of the day.

Once outside playing time was over, Grandma Joyful would tell Purr-Fect to come back inside the house. Purr-Fect would always obey her command because he knew that Grandma Joyful would reward him with a treat once inside the house. Wow! How neat is this that you get rewarded for listening!

After the treat, Purr-Fect would lay in his cat bed and watch Grandma Joyful as she sewed clothes or watched her favorite TV shows. All the while, Purr-Fect would be moving his tail side to side or up and down as if to show that he was extremely happy. Grandma Joyful would look at him with loving eyes and would nod her approval. Both were extremely happy with each other. There was true love and respect in this house!

Sometimes, when grandma was sewing or watching her favorite TV shows, Purr-Fect would patrol the inside of the house for small creatures that did not belong inside. He was not afraid of spiders, ants or snails. If he saw any of these creatures, he would push them with his paw until he pushed them out of the house. Again, Purr-Fect did this because of the love Grandma Joyful gave him and he wanted to show he loved her a lot also.

When this chore of checking for unwanted creatures was done, Purr-Fect would return to Grandma Joyful's side and especially to her legs and rub and purr to show that he was happy and to show his love for her. This always pleased Grandma Joyful, and she always let him know that she loved him. Time and time again, she would prove it by picking him up, setting him on her lap, and speak kind and loving words to him. This was very enjoyable for both Grandma Joyful and Purr-Fect.

Grandma Joyful and Purr-Fect still live in the same house close to your house and mine. If you are lucky and see a Siamese cat with blue eyes, whitish, or gray hair with black legs, then you may be looking at Purr-Fect. If you take another look, you will see Grandma Joyful close by watching out for her child. Ask her about Purr-Fect, and you will realize the love she has for Purr-Fect.

Moral of this story is that if a cat and a cat owner can take care of each other through respect and love, imagine what God will do for us because He loves each one of us a lot. He loves us much more than the love Grandma Joyful and Purr-Fect have for each other. Trust in God and in His love, let Him take care of you!

Slow

Many moons ago, there lived a snail family close to your house and mine. Like most families, there was a mom snail who we will name Hurrie, a dad snail who we will name Crawler, and of course the baby snail who we will name Slow so that we can follow along and experience some of their life's experiences.

The snail family, which we will know as Hurrie, Crawler, and Slow lived under a big rock, which was located in the back yard. The snail family's house was also near a creek that always had water so they had to avoid the water as they could not swim.

One day, Slow told his mom, Hurrie, and dad, Crawler, that he wanted to go out and explore the area around their home. Slow wanted to do this all alone. Of course, Mommy Hurrie would not allow this to happen. She was being a normal and overly protective mother and was totally against Slow going out on his own. She started telling Slow of the many reasons why she would not allow him to go out into the world all by himself.

Slow was really set on going out by himself that he told his mom, Hurrie, that he was a big snail and could take care of himself. He also said that he needed to really do this so that he could see what is outside of his home and also learn how to take care of himself. Mom Hurrie realized that her little snail was growing up and knew that Slow had a point. Mom Hurrie told Slow that he needed to ask his father, Crawler, for permission to go outside on his own to explore the local surroundings. Mom Hurrie hoped Daddy Crawler would deny Slow to go out as she was still against the idea.

Slow approached Daddy Crawler and asked for his permission to go outside their house to do some lone exploring. This conversation between dad and son brought memories back to Daddy Crawler as he had also many moons ago approached his dad with the same request. Daddy Crawler, much to Mommy Hurrie's dislike, quickly approved to let Slow go out on his own, but under some conditions.

Daddy Crawler told Slow that he would allow his request if he paid attention and followed his instructions which were: (1) Stay away from and do not go near the creek; (2) do not go off too far that you lose your way back home; (3) do not get in too much of a hurry to explore and get too thirsty; (4) stay away from and all animals bigger than you; (5) watch for humans walking or running on pathways; (6) watch out for hungry birds so stay close to grass line; (7) after a while, stop and eat some grass, and drink some water off grass leaves; (8) mark your way as you go so that you can follow your trail back home; (9) start your trip back home early so that you get home before sundown; (10) be extremely careful out there and come home safely.

After Daddy Crawler had given his instructions to Slow and after going through these instructions again and again until Slow had memorized them was he allowed to start his journey. Slow was thrilled that his daddy and mommy had allowed him to go and explore his surroundings all by himself.

No sooner had Slow left his house under the big rock when he saw for the first time what was the creek, and out of curiosity, he wanted to get close to the creek to see the water flowing by. Slow was about to go near the creek when he remembered Daddy Crawler's instruction, which was stay away, and do not go near the creek. Slow knew he better pay attention and chose not to go near the creek. So off he crawled in the opposite direction.

Slow started to notice that above his house was a big tree that had some birdhouses on it, so he knew that if he could see this big tree with birdhouses on it, that his house was right below this tree. He would not get lost if he could remember this fact.

Slow was so thrilled that his heart was beating real fast, and he was crawling so fast that he was starting to feel tired, thirsty, and sick. Slow remembered what Daddy Crawler had said, which was to not get in too much of a hurry and get thirsty. Slow decided to just stop and rest, but when he stopped, he started to notice some big animals with four legs, teeth, and a big nose, which they used to come smell him. This frightened Slow, but he would not move at all until animals were gone.

Slow thought the danger had passed when, all of a sudden, he could sense movement below his feet, and when he looked, he could see people running straight at him. Slow wanted to hurry and get near the grass line like Daddy Crawler had instructed him, but Slow was named Slow for a reason. He was slow to get anywhere. Fortunately, for Slow, the runners missed stepping on him. Slow was very lucky this time.

Next test Slow had to pass was the hungry bird test. Slow had remembered what Daddy Crawler had told him about eating and drinking water from grass leaves, so he was doing just that when he noticed a dark figure had blocked the sun from him. Slow looked up and saw a big bird looking at him, or so he thought, so he became motionless and would not move at all. Slow was even afraid to breathe as he thought the big bird would see him breathing and hurt him.

The big bird, lucky for Slow, flew away, and Slow went back to eating. Slow thought he had already had enough excitement for one day, so he started to head home knowing that it would take him a while to get there. Keep in mind that Slow had not traveled very far as he was slow to get somewhere and would be slow to get back. He remembered the tree with the birdhouses, and once he noticed the tree, he started crawling back home.

Slow did not realize it was going to take him so long to get home and started thinking that he should have started much sooner as the sun was going down fast and it was already getting dark. For the very first time, Slow was afraid. Slow was not only afraid of his mommy and daddy, but also of this darkness that he could not see through. Slow was starting to panic when he saw that his Mommy Hurrie and Daddy Crawler had turned on their house light for him so that he could see and find his way inside his home. Slow was very pleased and thankful that he had such wonderful, caring, and loving parents. Slow had made his first exploring trip a safe success.

So, next time you go out by the big tree that has birdhouses on it and notice a big rock beneath or close by the tree, look closely. If you are lucky, you will see Slow being his slow self and you will see his mommy, Hurrie, and daddy, Crawler, close by caring for him.

Moral of this story is that God gave us His commandments, but allows us to explore the world as we want to, but that He will welcome us back home to Him no matter how fast or slow we are in coming home! God leaves the eternal light on for us so that we can find our way home. What joy there will be in heaven when we return home. Greater joy than when Slow returned home to his parents! Enjoy life, but remember to come to God and come home!

Bunnie

Many moons ago, there was a small farm located real close to your house and mine. Being out in the country real close meant that you could walk to visit your neighbor even though they could not hear you if you shouted real loud, but in the country, this was considered close. This particular farm was owned by Mr. D Farmer and his wife, Clairy Farmer. Both Mr. D and Clairy were retired and had been for quite some time. Both had white hair and did not get around too quickly, but both knew how to plant a good garden and get great vegetables out of their garden.

They took great pride in their garden and planted all kinds of good eating stuff like tomatoes, carrots, lettuce, cucumbers, celery, okra, and cabbage. They planted all these vegetables that they liked to eat, so they watered them and kept a real close eye on them so that worms or other animals would not destroy their prized crop. As you can probably guess, Mr. D and his wife, Clairy, spent most of their day in the garden. You could see them weeding and turning the soil and watering their plants on a constant basis. They even spoke to their plants assuring them that they would take good care of them and all they had to do was give them good vegetables to eat.

One day, as they were in the garden, they noticed that some leaves were missing from their lettuce and cabbage plants. They also noticed that some carrots were missing. Mr. D asked his wife if she had picked some of these plants, and she said that she had not picked any of the plants he asked about. Mr. D started thinking that maybe the kids from two farms down the road had gotten into his vegetables. Mr. D could not think of any other reason why someone had taken only some pieces of his lettuce and cabbage and some whole carrots.

He had to get to the bottom of this as he could not afford to have his crop lost or stolen. Mr. D came up with a plan. He decided he would leave the porch light on at night so that the light would light up the garden. He would sit in the dark corner of the porch and wait and see if the thief or thieves came back to steal from his garden. Mr. D had decided to do this every night until he found who or what was taking his vegetables. It was on the third night that Mr. D got a glimpse of the thief. Mr. D spotted a big and fat rabbit that could barely move or hop. This particular rabbit was named Bunnie and had gotten so fat that she would not go with the other rabbits to eat in the meadow. Bunnie thought, *Why go far when we have all these delicious vegetables so close to our rabbit home?* Bunnie was a lazy rabbit, but she ate well and kept her strength by eating vegetables. Bunnie knew how to eat healthy.

Mr. D and Clairy were animal lovers, so getting rid of the rabbit was not an option. Mr. D advised Clairy that they would build a fence around their garden to keep this big, fat rabbit out of their vegetables. Bunnie heard what Mr. D said about her and was offended. She was so mad that she wished she could go into the garden right then and eat all the vegetables there. Bunnie's feelings were hurt. Mr. D told Clairy that he would go into town and the local feed store and buy some chicken wire, which should keep the big, fat rabbit out of the garden. Bunnie again heard how Mr. D described her and was pretty upset that he was calling her big and fat even though Bunnie admitted that he was right. All the other rabbits inside the rabbit house also called her big and fat, but Bunnie paid them no mind just as she had decided to pay Mr. D's comments about her no mind either.

When Mr. D came back from the feed store, he had all the material he needed to build the chicken wire fence and commenced immediately to get the fence in place. As mentioned above, they loved their garden and especially the vegetables their garden provided. Mr. D was going to keep any and all animals away from his garden and more importantly his vegetables. Mr. D and Claire were admiring the fence that they had built around the garden. Guess who else was watching the fence around the garden? You are right. Bunnie was also looking at the fence and kept thinking that she would not fit in-between the wire fence openings, and she was right. Bunnie had another plan. Bunnie decided to dig under the fence so that she could continue eating healthy by eating vegetables. Bunnie started to dig that very day, but keep in mind that she was totally out of shape as she had not exercised properly to keep her muscles strong. Bunnie had eaten healthy but had ignored the need to run around, walk, and jump as normal rabbits do to stay trim and strong. Bunnie liked to eat and not exercise, at least not exercise too much.

It took Bunnie two full days to get under the garden, and by that time, she was weak and very hungry, so she rewarded herself to some fresh homegrown carrots. Matter of fact, she ate seven carrots just to satisfy her hunger. Mr. D, in the meantime, was happy that, for two days, he had not seen any rabbits or any other animal in his garden. He padded himself on the back for putting up a very good fence to keep any animal out of the garden. Mr. D was weeding in his garden and happened to be in the area of his beautiful carrots when he noticed that some carrots were missing. How could that be Mr. D thought? I have not seen any animals or humans in my garden so what happened to my carrots?

It was not long before he got his answer. Mr. D was scratching his head and looking at his carrots when he noticed some dirt moving and then all of a sudden he saw the head of an animal he knew quite well. Can you guess whose head this was? You are right. Bunnie had blown her cover. She was caught in the act of stealing carrots from the garden. Mr. D had to do something but what could he do? He was still thinking about what to do when he heard his wife, Clairy, scream for help. The scream startled Mr. D and Bunnie, and both looked in the direction of Clairy. They both could see that Clairy was trying her best to walk or run fast to get away from something.

What was scaring her? Remember both Mr. D and Clairy were getting up there in their age, so their movements were slow and running was not an option. Mr. D called out to his wife that he was going to help her, but was having trouble walking in the garden. Bunnie was big and fat, but remember also that she had not eaten properly for two days so she had lost some weight. Bunnie came out of her rabbit hole and ran straight at Clairy. Bunnie did not know what danger she would face once there, but she knew she had to help Clairy. Once

Bunnie got close to Clairy, she saw what the danger was. It was a big and ugly poisonous snake that likes to eat rabbits and can also hurt humans. Bunnie was scared, but she used her speed and jumping ability to get the snake to change direction and not follow Clairy anymore.

The snake was willing to change direction now that he had dinner right there in front in the form of Bunnie. The snake would strike at Bunnie, but Bunnie was so quick and jumped real high that she never got bitten. She kept running and jumping at the snake's tail and then running away. She kept doing this until the snake thought he'd had enough of this crazy rabbit. The snake went out of the garden through a hole under the fence and kept on crawling at a fast pace away from the garden and this crazy rabbit. Mr. D, in the meantime, had reached his wife Clairy and both saw how Bunnie had saved them. They were glad that Bunnie had been around and inside the garden at this very moment.

Bunnie had made good friends on this day as he heard Mr. D tell Clairy that they should not worry about losing some of the vegetables to Bunnie as they had too many vegetables, and he could not think of a better person or animal to share their vegetables with. Bunnie also agreed with his comment.

Next time you are out in the country and notice that there is a vegetable garden, you may want to ask permission to look at the garden. Who knows, you may just be lucky enough to be in Mr. D's and Clairy's garden, and if you are extremely lucky, you may get a glimpse of Bunnie eating her vegetables. One more thing, just do not call her big and fat as she hates to be called that.

Moral of this story is that kindness should always be rewarded with true generosity.

Under normal circumstances you could not get Bunnie to attack a snake that likes to eat rabbits. But this meek, maybe big and fat, rabbit decided to help Clairy and Mr. D while risking her own life. It is written in the Bible. "The meek shall eat and be satisfied; they shall praise the Lord that seek Him, your heart shall live forever." Let's all be just like Jesus. Jesus came into the world, not as a weak person, but as a meek person. Be meek, be humble, seek the Lord and constantly praise the Lord! Store your treasures in heaven!

Mockey Jr.

Many moons ago, there was a mockingbird couple that built a nest in a near-by tree. The tree that the mockingbirds chose is in-between your house and ours. For the sake of this story, we will name the daddy mockingbird Mockey and the mommy mockingbird, we will name her Beattie so that we can follow some of their life experiences.

Mockey and Beattie knew that it was getting time to raise a family, so they both pitched in to gather twigs, grass, and any other material they could find and carry to build their nest or future home for their baby mockingbird. Early in the morning and late into the evening, you could see these two parents flying and hopping everywhere to get needed supplies for their nest. It was a sight to see how much energy they had as they built their nest.

They rarely stopped to eat as they had to finish the nest so that Beattie could lay her egg or eggs. As mentioned above, Mockey and Beattie had chosen the tree in-between our houses because we constantly fed wild birdseed to the local birds. Mockey and Beattie knew that they would never run out of food because of this fact, and they also knew that they did not have to go far and leave the nest unattended for long periods of time. This was an ideal place to build their nest, and they were taking great pride to build a strong and beautiful nest. It was not long before the nest was in place and built to Beattie's liking. As you know, the mommy in all cases gets the last word on how her house will be built and how it will look. Beattie was just being a normal mommy and wanted only the best for her little bird family.

Day finally arrived when Beattie laid inside the nest and laid one sole egg. Beattie was getting up in her age, so all she could lay was one egg. Mockey, once he saw that Beattie had laid one egg, was really excited and started hopping from branch to branch and chirping as loud as he could. Mockey wanted all the other birds to know that, soon, he would be a father. Beattie just looked at Mockey and smiled and shook her head at how Mockey was acting. Beattie also knew that Mockey was getting up in age, but today, he was not showing his age. Mockey was being very hyper and silly is what Beattie thought.

Beattie had to sit on the egg to keep it warm and to keep the sun from burning the egg. Mockey was in charge of bringing food to Beattie as she laid on the egg. Mockey brought Beattie all kinds of goodies that he caught such as worms, snails, butterflies, and cater-pillars. The food that Mockey brought to Beattie was full of vitamins, which would help keep Beattie in good health as she laid on the egg for very long periods of time. Mockey did not like to sit on egg but once again—what mommy says is what goes.

Beattie let Mockey know when it was his turn to lay on egg so that she could fly and stretch her wings and legs. Beattie also used this free time for grooming herself. She would fly to a local pond and bathe. Beattie loved being in the water as it made her feel good and refreshed her feathers and skin. Beattie would also eat any insect that she could catch when she was away from the nest, but she never told Mockey that she had eaten so Mockey was always worried that Beattie had not eaten. It was going real good for this mockingbird family and their egg until, one day, when a cat noticed the nest and climbed the tree to get to the nest and of course Beattie and the egg. Beattie was fully aware of the cat and would not breathe or blink an eye, so that the cat would not see her and her nest, but it was too late. Once the cat started climbing, the fight was on.

Beattie left the nest and chirped an alarm that Mockey heard and immediately flew toward the nest. When Mockey got there, he noticed that Beattie was putting a hurt on the cat as she was flying at the cat and pecking real hard at him. The cat probably thought there were ten birds attacking him instead of one mad mommy. Mockey almost stopped from helping Beattie fight the cat as he was enjoying seeing Beattie put a hurt on the cat, but he knew if he did not help that Beattie would take her anger on him so he joined in the fight.

Once Mockey got involved, the cat knew he was in deep trouble and ran down the tree and the yard. Cat wanted no part of mommy and daddy mockingbird or their family. Once all things went back to normal, Beattie still scolded Mockey as she thought he had not responded to her call for help quick enough. Mockey just shook his head and let her have the last word as he knew he would not win this argument. Mockey was a smart daddy and had learned well as he got older. On another occasion, while Beattie laid on her egg sound asleep, Mockey noticed a big snake crawling toward Beattie and their egg. Mockey went into attack mode. Mockey was going to protect his wife and his future family at all cost. Mockey let out a real loud alarm and flew straight at the snake in the tree. Mockey pecked as hard as he could on the snake's tail.

This hurt the snake, and it turned direction to confront Mockey. Mockey was not afraid and kept diving and pecking as hard as he could at the snake and never would get too close to the snake's mouth. Beattie, after Mockey sounded his alarm, was fully aware of the fight Mockey was in and stayed on top of the egg instead of joining Mockey in this fight. Beattie was going to protect the egg at all cost, but she kept a watchful eye on the fight between Mockey and the snake. Beattie thought for a while that Mockey was actually enjoying himself and showing off for her, and the best part is that Mockey was showing off for his wife.

Eventually, the snake was pecked at so much that the snake was hurting and decided that this was one fight that it would not win, so the snake hurriedly crawled off the tree and quickly slithered out of the yard. Mockey had won and protected his family, but his celebration was short lived. Beattie scolded Mockey for taking too long to convince the snake to leave the tree. Again, Mockey knew it was best not to argue. There were other occasions where Mockey and Beattie had to defend themselves and their home. One occasion was with a hawk that loves to eat mockingbirds and mockingbird eggs, but the hawk was no match for these protective parents. Another occasion was with a little boy that wanted to take the egg from its nest, but again the proud and protective parents scared the little boy, and he never came back to the nest again.

There was never a dull moment before the little mockingbird was born. Beattie and Mockey took turns feeding the little mockingbird, which they named Mockey Jr. Mockey, the dad, was thrilled to have had a son and that he would be named after him, so he vowed to take real good care of his son. Mockey Jr. was always hungry and kept crying for more and more food. This kept Mockey and Beattie extremely busy, but they never complained as their love for their son was great. Mockey Jr. finally grew feathers and learned to fly and speak in mockingbird language, so one day, he had a serious discussion with his mom and dad. Mockey Jr. wanted to know how he was born and what his mom and dad did prior to his birth. Mockey Jr. wanted to know if they had any problems protecting him prior to his birth.

Beattie and Mockey Sr. just looked at each other and told Mockey Jr. that there had been no problems and that all they did day after day was protect him when he was inside egg. They just stayed close to the egg and lovingly looked at the egg waiting for the baby to break the egg. Mockey Jr. said he was glad that protecting him had not brought them any problems or trouble. Mockey Sr. and Beattie just looked at each other and smiled. It's been a while since Mockey Jr. was born, so now he is flying, catching his own meals, and looking for his own girlfriend.

So, next time you see a big, handsome, and well-groomed mockingbird you may just be looking at Mockey Jr. If he is acting hyper and silly, he probably got that from his daddy. If he is acting responsibly and giving orders, he probably got that from his mom.

Watch Mockey Jr., but give him space so that you do not scare him away.

Moral of this story is twofold—first is that any parent will do anything to protect their family. Fear does not come into play when parents protect and defend their loved ones. Love dominates how the parents react to any problem. Secondly is that God said, "Look at the birds of the air; they do not sow or reap or store away in barns, and yet your Heavenly Father feeds them. Are you not much more valuable than they?" God will protect us constantly and He knows no fear! Put your trust in God!

Sport, Lylac, and Gill

Many moons ago, in a house not too far from your house and mine, lived a little boy and his little sister. Mom for these two children was named Merrie, and the dad was only known as Mr. Grubb. Little boy was named Sport, and his little sister was named Lylac. Remember their names so that you and I can follow some of their life experiences. Late one afternoon, Mr. Grubb told his two children that he would take them fishing tomorrow if they wanted to go. Lylac was not overly excited about the fishing trip, but said that she really wanted to go. Lylac, being just three years old, did not really get to fish on her own, so she spent most of the time looking for shells or throwing pebbles at little fish as they swam by.

She enjoyed being outside and close to the water in her bathing suit. Sport, being five years old, on the other hand, was really glad and screamed a very loud, "Yes!" Sport said that he could not wait to go fishing tomorrow.

The fishing plan was in place, and the only reason Merrie was not invited is that she had to work tomorrow. Sport was so excited that he told his dad that he was going to bed early so that he could get up early tomorrow. Sport wanted to head out to their favorite fishing spot real early in the morning, and he was not going to be the one holding them back in the morning, or so he thought. As stated above, Sport was so excited that he did go to bed early, but he could not fall asleep. He tossed, turned, and counted sheep in his mind over and over again, but he was so excited for morning to come that he could not fall asleep. Try as best he could, he was awake way past his normal bed time. It had not done Sport any good to have gone to bed early.

Seemed like Sport had just fallen asleep when he could hear his dad calling him by name and shaking his body so that he would wake up. Sport finally opened his eyes and realized that he was holding the fishing trip back. Sport jumped out of bed and headed straight to the bathroom where he washed his face, brushed his teeth, and combed his hair. Once he had done all that, he dressed himself with the clothes his dad had set out for him. Sport normally would complain, be lazy, and argue when he was told to get out of bed, but today, there was no time to complain as he was going fishing. Sport, on his way out of the house, grabbed and placed his favorite cartoon character cap on his head.

Sport was ready and just knew that today, he was going to catch all kinds of big fish that they could bring home to eat. Excited was not really a word we can use to show how pleased Sport was this morning. Dad's, Mr. Grubb's, truck finally arrived at their favorite fishing hole, and now it was time to catch all those hungry and good eating fish. Sport was the first one out of the truck, followed by Lilac, and climbed on the truck bed to get his fishing rod and reel. Lylac made a dash for the water's edge to see if she could see any small fish swimming near the shoreline. Mr. Grubb, being much older, moved a lot slower, but with better intentions and less wasted effort. Mr. Grubb told Sport to slow down or he could get hurt and warned Lylac not to get into the water. No exceptions!

It wasn't long before Sport landed his first little fish that was not big enough to keep to eat. Sport unhooked the little fish, studied the little fish, and noticed that he was having trouble breathing out of the water. Sport also noticed that the little fish's tail had been bitten in half by a larger fish. He also noticed that part of the fin behind his gill was also bitten in half. Poor little fish had been bitten bad, and now Sport had caught him. Sport thought that this was one very unlucky little fish.

Sport kept looking at the little fish he was holding in his hands when he thinks he could hear the little fish say, "Please, mister, let me go, put me back in the water before it's too late." You see, today is my birthday, and my parents let me swim alone as a present to me. They warned me not to eat anything without them being with me and for me not to swim too far from home. Right now, my mom is making some sardine cookies and shrimp pie to eat at my birthday party, so please, mister, place me back in the water so that I can go home. My parents are probably worried about me and are probably looking for me this very moment. Please let me go, and I'll always remember you for your kindness on each and every birthday that I have. By the way, mister, my name is Gill."

Sport was in shock that the little fish could talk or that he understood fish language. Sport decided right then and there that he would listen to the request the little fish made to him. Sport started heading toward the water's edge when he heard his dad, Mr. Grubb, tell him not to get too close to the water and especially not to get into the water. Sport looked at his dad and told him that he would be careful and would listen to his instructions. Sport knelt down at the water's edge and placed the little fish in the water, but before he released the little fish, Sport pulled and pulled the little fish back and forth so that water could go thru the little fish's gills. The little fish started to get his strength back and wanted Sport to turn him loose so that he could swim back home.

Sport finally released the little fish, and Gill was gone in an instant or Sport so thought. Gill swam back and eased his head above the water and told Sport, "Thank you," and also that he would come by on different days to the water's edge to see if he, Sport, was fishing. Sport and Gill were now lifelong friends. Mr. Grubb called out to Sport and asked him if everything was all right as he was not fishing anymore. Mr. Grubb could not see or hear Gill, so he was worried that his son was not having fun and was ready to go home. Quite the opposite, Sport was having a wonderful time as he had made a new friend and had in reality saved his life. Sport was also very pleased that Gill would get to enjoy his birthday party and eat some of the sardine cookies and shrimp pie that his mom had made for him.

Right before Gill swam off, he turned sideways and waved a goodbye with half of his remaining fin. Sport also waved his goodbye, wished Gill a very happy birthday, and told Gill to be careful of bigger fish that want to hurt him. Told him to always be on guard and avoid bigger and mean fish.

Who knows, next time you see a little boy fishing, you may just be looking at Sport. Look around the area Sport is in, and you may see his little sister, Lylac, playing near the water's edge. Look closer, and you will see Mr. Grubb fishing, but really keeping an eye on his two children. That is what parents do. Get a chance and you may want to get close to Sport and see if you get a glimpse of Gill. Good luck!

Moral of this story is twofold—one, we must always listen to our parents advise and follow their instructions. By doing this, we will stay out of trouble. Gill was very lucky that he met Sport and not someone else that may not have placed him back in the water. It would have been a very sad day and party for Gill's mom and dad if Gill had not gone home. Gill's mom and dad hugged and kissed Gill when he returned home, but Gill never told them that he had not followed their instructions. Gill had learned his lesson and would always do what his parents said. Two, Gill had some missing body parts, but had learned to survive with his missing body parts. Gill was not perfect, but he was alive and that is the main point of this story.

God loves us the way we are. We may not be perfect and may not always listen, but God will always release us to go our own way time and time again. If only we could learn from Gill and seek God as Gill vowed to seek Sport. Make time, seek Him, find Him, and let Him work!

Wagatail

Many moons ago, there lived a young boy and his best friend, which happened to be his puppy. We will name the little boy Ladder and the little pup, Wagatail, so that we can follow along with their life's experiences.

Ladder did not go anywhere without his best friend, Wagatail, by his side. Ladder could not imagine life without his best friend there beside him. I imagine that Wagatail also felt this way about his best friend and master. They were inseparable. Wagatail accompanied Ladder to their favorite fishing hole, to the amusement park in town, and even to the local grocery store. People that knew Ladder always looked for Wagatail beside Ladder as they knew they did everything together.

Only place Wagatail was not allowed to go was the school classroom, but Wagatail was not barred from the school grounds, so guess where Wagatail was while Ladder was in class? You are correct. Wagatail would sit under one particular tree close to Ladder's classroom and wait for his best friend and master to come out. You could almost feel the respect and love Ladder and Wagatail had for each other.

On weekends, Ladder had plenty of time to spend with Wagatail, so he decided to train Wagatail with the normal things that puppies get trained to do. First, Wagatail was taught to sit, which he mastered within hours. Wagatail sensed that if he obeyed and learned, his best friend and master would be real proud of him, so he did his best to learn and apply his learnings. Next came to lay down, which Wagatail understood the command and quickly obeyed. His best friend and master was so happy that he would give Wagatail a cookie treat once he learned and obeyed a certain command. Wagatail thought this was a fun game because he was getting a treat to do what he would do for his best friend and master even if he did not get a treat.

Next came lay down and roll, bark on command, shake hands, jump, chase tail, and ultimately fetch ball or stick thrown by his best friend and master. Wagatail passed all these tests—thumbs up. There was not anything he would not do for his best friend and master. Besides, he was still getting cookie treats. Who in the world would not learn or work for cookie treats?

One day, as Ladder and Wagatail were running in a local pasture, Wagatail had an incident. Wagatail had jumped over a log, landed on uneven ground, and hurt his foot. Ladder knew Wagatail was hurt by the loud yelp Wagatail let out and then by sitting on the ground while holding his front leg up. Ladder called out to Wagatail to come to him, but Wagatail would not move. Wagatail was in pain.

Once Ladder realized that Wagatail could not walk, he decided that he would carry his best friend, Wagatail, back home so that he would not get hurt any more than what he was already. Ladder thought that carrying Wagatail was the logical thing that a caring best friend and master could do. So, Ladder carried Wagatail all the way home while all the time hugging, kissing, and speaking sweetly and softly to Wagatail. Their friendship was forever set in concrete after this occurrence.

Once Ladder arrived at home with Wagatail in his arms, he rushed in the door and told his mom that Wagatail was hurt and needed to see a doctor. Ladder even said that he had some money stored away that could be used to pay the doctor. Such was the love between Ladder and Wagatail.

Mom touched Wagatail's paw, and he winced and cried out in pain, so mom agreed with Ladder that Wagatail had to see a pet doctor so it was off to the local veterinarian. Once they arrived, the doctor took Wagatail to one of the rooms to examine Wagatail. Doctor was very good at being a doctor, but you could tell that Wagatail was hurt because he would cry out when his hurt paw was touched.

After careful examination and applying a few tricks that the doctor knew, he finally told Ladder and his mom what was wrong with Wagatail's paw. Doctor said it was not serious, but that he needed to remove a big tree splinter that was inside Wagatail's paw. Said it may hurt him for a while, but once I pull splinter, he will be relieved and the pain will go away.

Sure enough, once the splinter was pulled, Wagatail was his normal self. Wagatail started licking all of us and especially the doctor for helping him, but he was truly grateful to his best friend and master for carrying him out of the pasture, bringing him home, and bringing him to the vet clinic. Not to mention that Wagatail had heard that Ladder would use his saved money to pay the doctor that treated him. Such loyalty from two best of friends—one, a puppy, and one, an owner and master of the puppy.

Ladder and Wagatail are now back home doing what best friends do, which is taking care of each other, playing alongside each other, sleeping in the same room, and sometimes eating out of the same plate. That's what true friends do!

If you are lucky, you may see a young boy teaching his puppy new tricks, and just maybe you may be looking at Ladder and Wagatail having fun and getting closer to each other.

Moral of this story is that if a puppy can learn new tricks and apply learnings to satisfy and gratify his owner and master, imagine how much joy we would bring to our Owner and Master if we could show Him the respect, love, and loyalty that Wagatail showed to Ladder. Believe in our God and Master because he will always be with us. Believe me, our God is trying to teach us, but we do not learn as quickly as Wagatail did. Give thanks to our Master for being so patient with us!

Wormy

M any moons ago, there lived a worm inside a real big, firm, and extremely red apple. We will name this worm Wormy so that we can follow Wormy's life experience.

One day, Wormy was resting after eating and cleaning some of the inside of the apple, Wormy was resting as anyone that has ever eaten or bitten into a very good, firm, and juicy apple knows that it takes an effort to truly enjoy an apple . . . Wormy was no exception. Eating was work!

No sooner had Wormy dosed off for his usual four-hour nap when Wormy felt his house (apple) violently move. This violent move, not only woke him up, but it also caused Wormy to slither to the opening Wormy had made on the apple to see what had caused his house to move so violently.

Just as soon as Wormy poked his head outside the apple did he notice that something with teeth had bitten into his apple and had pulled the apple from the apple tree. It took Wormy a while to figure out who owned those teeth. Wormy had to crawl out of the apple and then climb on top of the lips of this animal. Finally, when Wormy had made his way above the teeth, lip, and up the animal's nose did Wormy realize that the thief was a horse. Wormy called the horse a thief as the horse was stealing his house.

Wormy hollered at the horse to stop what he was doing and especially to quit biting into his house. The horse was stunned to see this worm on top of his nose and especially that he could understand what Wormy was saying. The horse stopped chewing the apple and gently placed the apple on the ground.

Wormy thanked the horse for listening to his plea and offered to be his best friend if the horse granted one more favor. The horse asked Wormy what he needed and said he would do his best to grant Wormy's wish.

Wormy told the horse that if the apple was left on the bottom of the tree that other animals would come and eat up his house. Wormy even said that a worse case event would be that someone or another animal might come by and trample his house with him in it. Not good for Wormy!

Horse asked Wormy how he could help him. Wormy told horse to place apple up on the apple tree in a place that the wind would not knock the apple off the apple tree. Wormy told the horse to stretch out his neck and place the apple as high as he could, but before he did that, Wormy had to get back into his apple house.

Once the apple was set up on the apple tree and all was secure, Wormy poked outside the apple's opening and thanked the horse for listening to him. Both Wormy and the horse went their different ways, and Wormy resumed his much needed nap knowing full well that once he woke up, he was going to have to clean up the mess of seeds within the apple that had been scattered when apple was violently moved. But Wormy decided that naptime was more important than cleaning house.

Wormy enjoyed the remainder of his Wormy life and eventually left his apple house when he grew wings and outgrew his home.

Look closely at a butterfly you see floating in the air, and if you are lucky, you may just see Wormy enjoying his new life!

Moral of this story is that no matter how violent your life may be shaken, God is with and by you to pull you through and out of troubling times. Enjoy life, and let Him lead!

Patriotic

American Proud

Thank God for this country
Thank God for the military men and women
That protect us here and over seas
That protect our precious freedom

As a youngster I always stopped and watched
A commercial about our military men and women
I would always salute these brave men and women
While clutching my reliable Daisy BB gun

I remember my brother Bob volunteered to be a Marine
Jose, Pancho, Fred, Mary, and Tramaine also left our town
The Army was calling and they had to see the world
They all left with a smile and nary a frown

The German's son down the road from us also left
But also the Irish young man beside the German's farm
Come to think of it so did the pretty Italian girl
Along with the native Indian man named Little Big Horn

They all joined the Navy and will be patrolling the seas
But we also had some join the Air Force as they wanted to fly
I remember Aziz, Martin, and Shanika all wanted to soar
Above the clouds patrolling the sky

The Polish and Czech family also sent their sons
The Japanese mother cried when her daughter went away
But she said to her mother—I have to serve my country
You'll be proud of me when I come home to stay

It's really amazing to see how different this group was
We had Americans, Canadians, Britons, Muslims, Germans, and
Mexicans
Native Indians, Italians, Japanese, Hispanics, Afro Americans, Polish,
Irish, and Czechs
But bottom line these were all red blooded and proud Americans

I salute them all and pray for their safety and protection
salute all past and present military men and women
Remember one thing—I, along with other races I failed to mention
Are very proud Americans—and I have your back— me and my
trusted Daisy BB gun

Welcome Home

B anners briskly waving in the air marking the path of the wind
National flags proudly displayed for all the world to see
Friends and family joyfully gathered to spend some quality
time together
Meat on the pits and all this was sincerely and lovingly meant for me

I made my rounds and saw places I'd never would have visited or seen
I proudly wore my colors and we never backed down from any threat
I was part of a fraternity, brotherhood, or caring and supportive family
That honored our democracy and any resistance—dead on we met

But now after more than twenty years of dedicated and honorable
service
I left my fraternity, brotherhood and supportive family behind
I will miss all my superiors or subordinates that I got to know real
well
They know I served with the utmost respect and pride, and I am sure
they do not mind

It's nice to be back home and to be honored for the work I did at
home and abroad
For the multiple tours of hazardous duty that I was assigned and that
were completed
All because of my comrades that always had my back no matter the
situation
I proudly salute my comrades as I look at our platoon picture with
me in it

Such pride, strength, unity, loyalty, honor, and absolute precision
Was clearly displayed as various hostile locations we meticulously
    roamed
Such was the life I led for the last 20 plus years and have no regret
But you know—I thank my God for bringing me safely back home

I've made the full circle and now I will have to adjust to the pace at
    home
I'll fit into society and hopefully I'll get back with old friends and
    family too
I'll proudly retire my service uniforms and metals and all the awards
    I received
Retire my old, dusty, and well broken in boots and buy some tennis
    shoes

I never cried while I was away and danger was prevalent with every
    step we took
But seeing those banners waving along with Old Glory proudly wav-
    ing everywhere
Was really humbling and inspiring—a little bit too hard for me to
    take
I could honestly feel the love from all the people gathered here and
    there

Tears just started flowing the minute I saw mom, dad, brothers, and
    some of my friends
Felt all their love and respect, my tears I did not hide but wanted
    them to see
I wanted them to know that I missed them too and felt proud to be
    back home
And to show them that I truly enjoyed this reunion meant especially
    for me

The central theme from all who greeted me was glad you are back, "Welcome home"

And thanking me for all the years I helped protect my home and country

For keeping us safe and fighting any and all injustice all over the world

For standing up for righteousness—standing up for true democracy

I made my rounds and while I was away I prayed a lot and always had Him with me

Cradled and prayed to my God on a constant basis no matter where I was sent to roam

Now fully realize that not only on earth will there be joy about my safe return

But a big and joyous party in Heaven when I am greeted with the words, "Welcome Home"

Christian Life

Angels Amongst Us?

One hot summer morning, I decided I'd do some exercising by jogging around our neighborhood. As I stepped outside the house, the strangest thought invaded my mind. I was bewildered yet curious that this thought would cross my mind, especially at a time when I was getting ready to jog and my mind would be totally occupied on that task.

To reiterate, I was bewildered yet curious enough to try to answer the question posed to my feeble mind, which was, "Are there really angels amongst us?" I decided to tackle this question through normal reasoning and hopefully my decision would be based without any bias to my Christian belief. I was mulling my course of action as I stretched for my neighborhood run.

As if by divine intervention, I started my jogging run without reaching a conclusion or being anywhere close to submitting a well thought out or intellectual answer to the question at hand. My mind was now occupied with my surroundings, traffic, and potential places that I needed to avoid to keep from spraining an ankle or worse. I was in exercise—forget everything else mode.

I had not jogged a couple of blocks when I noticed poor Miss Miller getting groceries from her car and taking them inside her house. Miss Miller was a well-respected elderly woman that lived alone and always greeted friends or strangers. I believe Miss Miller did not know what a stranger was. Anyway, I noticed she had numerous grocery bags that she had to take inside the house, and I noticed that she was having trouble with the bag she currently carried. I called out to her while at the same time rushing to grab the bag she was carrying. I told her I would unload the remaining groceries and that she need not worry about anything except putting up groceries. I even asked her if she needed help doing that. She declined my offer to help put up groceries, so once I unloaded her groceries and locked her car, I was back to getting my exercise in.

A block or so from Miss Miller's house, I came upon a little boy that had fallen off his bike. The child was crying and appeared to be hurt, but I could not see any broken bones or any evidence of blood. I asked the young lad to tell me where he was hurt and if he needed me to take him home. The young boy told me that his hurt was more inside and not outside, he said that if his father knew he had fallen off bike that his bike would be taken away. I told the boy that I agreed with him in so far as being hurt inside was much worse than any physical pain. He looked stunned by my words, but I went on to say that he and I had a secret that would never be revealed to anyone. He smiled, thanked me for my help, and got back on his bike with a big grin across his face. Come to think of it, I had that same grin on my face. I resumed my jogging session as soon as I saw the young lad would be all right.

Ironically, I had not jogged too far past my last stop when I noticed a very young girl trying to cross a very busy and dangerous intersection. Noticed that each and every time that she even contemplated crossing that cars would zip on by and blare their horns as a warning. I called out to this little girl and told her to let me help her get across the street. She was leery at first, but I assured her I meant her no harm and that I didn't want her to be hurt as she tried to navigate across this dangerous intersection. She finally accepted my help, and it seems like as soon as I volunteered that I would help her cross the street that the traffic died down drastically, and we were able to cross without being rushed or having any sort of incident. I watched this little girl go up her driveway, into her garage, and ultimately her house. Now, I was free to get back to jogging.

I had not even commenced to get into my jogging session when I heard a woman screaming. I noticed that her pet dog had pulled the dog leash from her hands and was running free alongside this very busy intersection, which, all of a sudden, had reverted to being extremely busy and drivers zipping by at a fast pace.

I ran toward her dog hoping that I wouldn't be bitten while trying to perform a good deed. Several cars blared their horns, but never reduced their speed as they almost ran over the dog. Fortunately, the dog would return to the same side of the street his owner and I were on. No telling what would have happened if he had tried to cross the street. I do not even want to think of that. I ran after the dog and was finally able to land a foot on the trailing leash. This stopped the dog's progress, and I reached down to grab the leash and proceeded to hand over this pet to its rightful owner. Woman was grateful and extremely happy that I had come along at this time and had saved her pet from potential injury or worse. As I resumed my jogging, I couldn't help but think of the alternative if I had not been there to help.

Seems like I should have jogged miles and miles as I noticed I had left the house quite some time back, but I had only jogged five blocks at the most. I decided to head back home. A couple of blocks up the road, two of my neighbor's kids were trying to get their soccer ball, which had rolled across the street. Keep in mind that this is the same street where drivers are in a hurry and seldom brake their vehicle, but readily blare their respective car horns when anything or someone wants to invade their lane of travel. I hollered at the young lads to hold tight and that I would retrieve their soccer ball. After some futile attempts and one too many near misses, I was finally able to retrieve the soccer ball, cross the street back to where the kids were, and handed over the soccer ball. I was glad that this situation was finally over.

By this time, I was so close to being home that I walked the remaining length. As I neared my walkway, that same question popped into my head again, "Are there really angels amongst us?" Weird that I started my exercise jog with this question and evidently was going to end my session with the same question. I am still bewildered and confused, and maybe later on or tomorrow, I will take the time needed to properly answer this question.

Believe in His Ways

As I walked into our small and humble church
I couldn't help but notice some kids playing on the street
Brought back memories of my youthful days
Back then I was pretty agile when I stayed on my feet

Such pleasant and sweet memories of yesteryear
When as a kid we had no worries and really nothing to fear
But reality struck and brought me back to the present time
Reminded me of why some force had brought me here

Inside the church I felt at ease as best I could
Been only days since I lost my best friend, my dad
Dad always brought us to church as a kid
Always said—come to the Lord with a smiling face and do not be sad

I couldn't help but think of dad's advice
But I broke down, cried out loud and buried my face in my hands
I'm glad that no one else was in the church
When I heard a young voice say—Father please help this man—amen

With teary eyes that made it real hard for me to see
I noticed a very young boy standing right beside me but on the
    church aisle
He asked me if he could help or if I just needed someone to talk to
I finally cleared my eyes enough to see that this young man had a
    big smile

He asked me if I needed a doctor as when you're hurt you cry
He asked if my stomach or head did hurt or if I was cut somewhere

He kept on asking me some questions that I forgot about my painful loss
He asked me why I came to church and not just anywhere

I tried to hold my tears from flowing freely in my eyes
I looked as this young boy and felt like he really understood
I told him my pain was coming from inside and something brought
    me here
He told me—maybe another angel was needed and that's why your
    father He took

His words hit home, and I cried and moaned out load
I felt the pain and again hid my face to drown out all the groans
Little boy touched and padded me on my back
When I looked up the little boy was no longer there, the little boy
    was gone

I quickly ran to see the kids playing outside
To see if this little boy was playing there
I looked and looked at all the kids and none reminded me of him
The little boy who had been with me was not close by or anywhere

I went back into the church to pray while still thinking of this young
    boy
I recollected how he made me feel at ease even though he was much
    younger than me
The little lad's prayer was so inspiring when he said, "Father, help
    this man"
Through teary eyes he stayed with me until my eyes cleared and I
    could see

I knelt down and thanked our God for sending His Son to be with me
I left the church really relieved and smiling as now I understood
Our God knows what He is doing, and He is always in control
He sends His son to explain why another angel He took

Come to the Country

Come to the country
And be my country man
Put on some country boots and try
To keep up with me if you can

I'd rather be in a pasture
Feeding all of the cows
Than walking a fancy mall
Doing nothing—just browsing around

I'd rather eat steak and potatoes
Served on a plain plate
Than watching a movie—eating out
And staying up late

I'd rather drive my tractor and
Plow up the land
Than sleep with air condition
Instead of my noisy fan

So come to the country
Come—if you can
Come to the country and be
My loving country man

Come to the country and be my country man
I know I'll make you happy—I know I can

Country Heaven

R iding down a country road
　　With no destination in mind
　　I pulled into a rustic country store
To see what I could find

The store was spotless and really nice
Cowboy pictures hanging on the wall
I tried to find who the artist was
When a voice asked—can I help you, sir?

I turned and noticed her deep blue eyes
Her shirt was plaid-pink, yellow, and blue
Her denim jeans fit exceptionally well
Which she tucked into her leather boots

I couldn't speak for quite some time
This girl was really quite a sight
I kept staring at her lovely auburn hair
When I heard her say—are you all right?

I finally got the strength to ask
Am I in Country Heaven?
She smiled and blushed and answered back
I guess we are cause now I am believing
That dreams do come true
Cause I've dreamt of meeting someone like you
And I hope we stay in Country Heaven

Country Roots

Oh how I miss my country farm and ranch
And riding old Buck through the pasture and up the hill
Or driving old reliable tracky as we plowed the pasture
Gathered hay bales or fixing the well

Of getting dirt inside my cowboy boots
Or stepping on something left behind
Of feeding the chickens, pigs, steers, and lambs
On getting up early to begin the daily grind

But things have changed when I topped the charts
I now ride a truck with four hundred horses
Tractors are nowhere to be seen
Instead of silence we hear cars, trucks and buses

I long to see and smell the chickens, pigs, steers, and lambs
But here I have to go to a petting zoo
People here do not know how to tend to a ranch
As country people learn to do

It's hard to get some dirt inside my boots
It's hard to see the stars at night
To sit outside without a care
Or hear a coyote as he welcomes the night

It's hard to complain about the life I lead
As I still wear my jeans and boots
I have all the money I could ask for
But I still miss my country roots

Dare to Dream

Seems just like yesterday I left my country home
I still remember the tears I shed as I left my best friend and
mom
The words that they said still cling to me and every day I hear them
say
Dare to dream and live the dream

The dream is now for real and the shows keep coming and coming
The audience keeps growing and growing and my songs are on fire
But deep down I still see my humble parents waving and saying
Dare to dream and live the dream

At every show I look up to heaven and thank my Lord
And ask that He take good care of mom and dad
I ask that He instill in them the basic thought they conveyed
Dare to dream and live the dream

The miles may separate us and keep us far apart
But our thought and prayers keep us close together
I thank you for your encouragement and still remember
Dare to dream and live the dream

Life has been good to me and really rough on you
I've come home to show my love and say goodbye
With teary eyes I cry out to you
Because of you I dared to dream and live my dream

Ever Wonder?

I 'm sure you've seen a homeless person somewhere in your town
Or a person asking for alms somewhere on the street
I'm sure you've noticed their poor attire and disheveled look
And I'm sure this person is one you'd rather not meet

You read their sign which generally states
I'm homeless, without work—please help me
You stare and generally roll up your car windows if you're alone
Thank the Lord that your kids were not with you to see

You utter something and try to neglect this human being
You finally get a green light and promptly speed away
You can't help but wonder why this person can't get a job
Why can't this person go away and not be there each and every day

Another thing I'm sure you've seen and probably more than once
An elderly couple at the grocery store with their attire not too neat
They venture down the grocery aisles, but seldom load their cart
Finally get to the meat section, look at prices and finally get a small
    package of meat

They get and buy what they can afford and nothing that is
    non-essential
Cart is loaded with only milk, bread, and some different cans from
    here and there
Makes you wonder what life they lead and how they make it through
You even wonder—why the disparity—why is life in their golden
    ages not fair

Here is another example of what we have seen and commented
    freely on
Unkempt kid with dirty and torn jeans—dirty shirt walking to school
Mingling with your kid in class and on the playground
Your kid with only the best clothes and shoes—looking real cool

I can go on and on, and I am sure you'll agree
Even at church you see the clothing gap—whether it be by ethnicity
You tend to judge those dressed poorly or maybe inappropriately
Utter within yourself—are you serious, really?

Or what about your trips to the hospital ever see this one?
People sleeping on hospital couches as they wait on loved ones
Again, you tend to judge their actions and really look for faults
You can't help but mumble—why can't these people move on?

Maybe I'll quit after we talk about this occurrence
Have you ever visited or talked about a person in prison?
Again, our judgmental self comes into the forefront
We state—I'm sure he is there for some good reason

But now that we have discussed the unpleasant things we see in life
Can you honestly tell me what Jesus looks like or how He will appear?
Will he be dressed like King Solomon in his entire splendor—fine
    jewelry and robes?
Or like John the Baptist—will His eyes look happy or will they be
    full of tears?

Will He be dressed as a homeless begging for help?
Or as a poor person at a grocery store, or a poor innocent kid going
    to school?
Or a person you judged that goes to your church or maybe the poor
    at the hospital?
Or the person in prison that was locked up and you thought was real
    cool?

You see, no one really knows how the Good Lord will test each one
of us

No one knows how and where He will appear—not the hour or the
moment

But if you want to change your ways and learn His lesson

In the bible read Matthew: Chapter 25 verse 31 thru 46 entitled
Final Judgment

So stop and think about what you say or do to those less fortunate
than you

This is your notice—food for thought or thoughts for you to ponder

Where or how will He appear and test your kindness?

Will you pass or fail His test—ever wonder?

Family

In my youthful years she guarded me without a fear
She played alongside of me and always had my back
She was my older sister—mentor and coach
She always took up for me, which made me real glad

She'd load me on our little red wagon and told me to hold tight
She would pull me up the hill and down the other side
I thought she was the strongest girl that ever, ever lived
Her strength and endurance were definitely out of sight

My sis would take me to the park and load me on a swing
And again she would give me instructions—don't move and hold on
    tight
She'd push the swing time and time again and seemed never to tire
She was my big sis, and she guarded me day and night

Those wonderful years of our youthful prime did not last
Next thing we knew we were both going to school
My big sis would walk me to school and wait to take me home
She was my hero and being with her I thought was real cool

We went through our elementary years without a hitch
And the same goes for our intermediate school years
We were family and took care of each other as best we could
When we were together, we definitely had no fear

By my high school years I had grown bigger and stronger than my sis
And now it was my turn to take care of her as best I could
I would defend her and take up her cause and would not falter
We were family and I did not appreciate it when others were rude

We made it through high school and sis graduated three years before
      me
At her graduation night or graduation party I cried a tear or two
I was so happy for her, but yet felt a deep void in my life
But that void was filled by playing football, baseball, and soccer too

My big sis was there to wish me well on my graduation night
I hugged her and thanked her for being my best friend
I vowed to take care of her as best I could
Cause that's what family does—love family until the end

I got a scholarship to go play ball at one of the big universities
And sister had found true love to marry our neighbor's son
They moved down the street from mom and dad's house
But sis always called when she found out we had won

I finally graduated from the university I attended
And really had a very illustrious sports career
The motivation I had throughout this campaign was
My sister in my youthful years saying—play without fear

The Lord blessed me totally beyond belief
For he sent an angel in the form of my sister to take care of me
He made me strong and kept me from getting hurt
And opened a door, which has allowed me to make lots of money

I wish I could say that this fairytale is without a hitch
But time and life takes its toll on everyone
Things that were are gone and only memories remain
Big sis to a massive stroke, she did succumb

Big sis can no longer do the things she used to do
She has to go places while sitting in her uncomfortable wheel chair
But guess who's pushing her every chance I get
Paying her back from our youthful years which is only fair

You see our family bond is beyond reproach
We are brother and sister until the very end
We will love and support each other as only family knows
We will always be there for each other—amen!

Give Me a High Five

In my youth I was considered, by all accounts, as being a normal kid
Little did those that truly know me understand that I was overly whimsical
My mind travelled at an unbelievable pace and always sought answers
Often times my unleashed curiosity was uncontrollable and truly quite comical

My quest for answers sometimes got me into trouble at home
But on this particular adventure, I am sure my parents would not mind
Mom and dad always told me about Jesus and about Heaven being above
I started searching for Jesus to see what ultimately I would definitely find

My first clue was that Jesus was in Heaven and lived with His Father there
But my parents always said that Jesus was with us and lived everywhere
They said He cared for the sick, young, and old, and always kept everyone safe
They said *He was a righteous God always kind, loving, caring, and fair*

The clues my parents gave me puzzled me and made my task a little harder
But I was told that when one leaves earth that Jesus meets that person in Heaven
That narrowed my quest and my feeble mind began to wander
My goal to find Jesus would be completed at my very tender age of seven

I started to question how I could reach the Heavens above
How could I get close to Heaven and reach out and touch our God?
And if I found God how would He react to my inquisitive nature?
Would He scold me, avoid me, give me a smile or give me an approving nod?

No sooner had I asked these questions when I had mastered a grand plan
I decided through common reasoning that my task was simple enough
Reasoning was that we lived down in the valley and Heaven was farther up from us
But climbing a big hill next to our home would get me real close to Heaven above

It was off to the races and up the very high hill I enthusiastically go
It took me a while to get to the top and noticed that Heaven had gone a lot higher
I sank down to my knees and started to weep and cried out to Jesus above
I cried—you know I wanted to meet you, that was my only quest—my only desire

But then out of nowhere He calmly and pleasantly spoke and said to me
He said, you do know Me and have met Me every time you look up at the sky
He said He was truly delighted to have met me and warned me never to tell
About the day I met Jesus, spoke to Jesus, and the day Jesus gave me a high five

I am sure Jesus has and will forgive me for the telling of our little secret
I am sure He takes into consideration that I was very young, just seven

But when I leave this earth and Jesus meets me in Heaven I will tell
Him
As a kid you gave me a high five, please let me enter into your home
in Heaven!

Giving Thanks for His Help

How great is thy love for us that you comfort us no matter if
we fail in Christian life
How wonderful is thy mercy that you ease our worries
before they become real
How powerful is thy healing grace that you start to heal us before
we ask
How beautiful are you my God—healing and lifting me—seems so
surreal!

You know where we are going and know where we have been
You always guard us no matter how we act, do, or say
You always rejoice when a sinner comes back home to you
Rejoice like the earthly father and prodigal son that returned after he
went away

Such joy there is in heaven when the 100th sheep is found
Or when the lamp is lit and the 10th coin is finally found
Or when thru your grace and power you open the eyes of the blind
Or open the ears of a person that has never in his life heard a sound

The lepers have been cured of all their sickness and curse
But only one came back to give you his thanks
But faith has always had its way and most did acknowledge your grace
Like the Roman centurion full of faith even though he was way up
in rank

But just like the boy afflicted with demons that you drove the demons
out
Or the hemorrhaging woman that was healed by touching your clothes

Your glory and grace is beyond our understanding
You healed all that you came in contact—healed all and not a few or
     most

And now that I have truly seen your power, healing grace, and love
I want to be like the person that was cured of his leprosy
I want to say You are truly my God and that I accept Jesus Christ
As my Lord and Savior and especially want to thank Thee!

Ask you Lord to keep on working thru me so that I can work for you
I will forever proclaim your glory, grace, and love in all that I do!

Goodbye

I still remember the day I left and recollect how proud I felt
I loved the way I was dressed and at how much effort was placed
to make me look my best
Loved the flowers and live plants aligned next to my new and eternal
home
Wished I could have smiled when pictures were taken as those mem-
ories will forever last

I especially loved the presence of all my family and really felt their
love for me
My heart was broken to see their teary eyes and to hear their desper-
ate sighs
Felt their anguish, pain and concern at my sudden and unexpected
departure
Heard them speaking to God and asking the common and universal
question—why?

Never in my wildest dreams would I have imagined that my depar-
ture would hurt so much
That my sons, daughters, spouse, brother, and sisters would miss me
so much
I can still feel their tears on my lifeless skin as they cried over me and
looked so hurt
I can still feel their pain, embraces, kisses, and more importantly
their loving touch

The funeral mass/service was divine and the kind words spoken filled
me with pride

Who could have imagined that my next to last farewell would be
   immaculate
I thank my God that He gave me such a caring, wonderful, and lov-
   ing family
Thank my God for being blessed beyond belief, that I was so truly
   fortunate

The trip to my eternal resting place was uneventful, but I could see
   the procession
The final farewell was just as sad for me as for all my family gathered
   there
I heard their moans, cries, and could see that some could not accept
   that I was gone
Their tears stained the earth and their clothing, there wasn't a dry eye
   anywhere

Again, as my earthly body was lowered to its final resting place
I kept looking at my family and still felt their grief and their desolate
   sigh
I remember thinking how desperate and lost I would have felt if the
   tables were turned
And to one of mine I was saying the final and inevitable goodbye

Time has passed us by, and I still think of how lovely my family
   looked on my last day
I miss them so much and wish that they take real good care of one
   another
I wish that they would come visit and spend some time with me, is
   that too much to ask?
Just sit with me, bring me music, their love, their stories, or simply
   one flower

Now, even though I have been gone for a while, I still miss my family
   as a whole
Wish that they would make time to come visit and spend some time
   with me

To just sit and talk or pray and tell me how things are going and how
they feel
To let me know they still love, miss me, and to let me know of addictions to our family tree

I guess life has to go on and sometimes it is hard to stop or leave the
world behind
I just wish that the love we shared had fallen on fertile ground and
taken deeper roots
Instead of falling on the trodden path where the seed was trampled
and ruined
Or on rocky ground where the seed sprouted but the sun dried up
the tender shoot

Now I know how our God must feel when we neglect to honor Him
on a constant basis
We do not make time to come visit Him at His house and there ask
for forgiveness and pray
Now I fully know how proud and glad our Father is when the prodigal son has returned
Came to visit, ask for forgiveness and to pledge loyalty and more
importantly to stay

I am not asking for much, and I do not expect you to go out of your
way
But I hope you come by to visit, and I truly hope it is today!

Hope

I finally got the courage to ask her to marry me
Promised to take care of her and never—never leave her side
The promise that I made to her will forever and ever stand
We would be happy living on my ranch—up on the countryside

She said she'd love to marry me but had a very good paying job
She was quickly going up the corporate ladder and doing very well
She didn't want to lose everything by moving to the country
Said, "how are you going to take care of me—please tell"

I said I have 375 acres that in 10 years will be mine
An old 1997 Ford pickup that runs most of the time
20 head of cattle and two bulls that roam that ranch of mine
An old 1980 tractor that runs most of the time
20 plus chickens that lay breakfast everyday
3 old roosters that wake me up each morning with their chickeedeedee
An old 3-bedroom house that sits way up on a hill
Leaks a little here and there but keeps out most of the chill

You see, I have a little bit to offer but none better than my heart
I have all I ever wanted but you are the missing part
If you do decide to marry me I'll name my ranch in your honor after
     you are mine
I'll even let you drive my old pickup and tractor that run most of the
     time

I see you have something to offer and I gladly accept your offer
And we can really make this marriage work with help from the Lord
     above

I really like the idea of naming the ranch after me—we'll divide the
    land in 3 pastures
One named Faith, middle named Hope after me, and the last one
    Love

We can and will make this marriage last with guidance from above
We will work the ranch together and lead a very good life
I vow to make you happy and to be a loyal, caring, and loving wife
And after we are married the ranch, chickens, bulls, cows will also
    be mine
Along with the old pickup and tractor that run most of the time

How Will I Go?

Ever wonder how you will go?
    Will sickness win the battle we are braced to fight?
    Ever wonder when your time will be up?
On your last breath, will there be darkness or will there be light?

Will pain dominate your body and mind?
Will I be surrounded by loved ones on my last day?
Will I be aware of what's happening to me?
Will my family let me go or demand that I be saved?

Will it be sudden, unexpected and pain free?
Or will it be expected but with lots of pain?
What will the weather be like on my last day?
Will it be cold, sunny or a day full of rain?

Which sickness have I chosen to fight?
Which sickness will be my plight?
Will I be able to see . . . to keep my sight?
Will the Doctors' diagnosis be right?

How long will I suffer before the end?
How much pain will I have to endure?
Will my mind be all there and understand?
For my sickness, will they ever find a cure?

Such silly things that dominate one's mind.
But this path we must all travel and that's a guarantee.
No need to worry about this uncontrollable matter.
No sense in running or to flee.

Our path is chosen and our future is set.
Our time is limited and not in our control.
The date and time will eventually get to us.
We may be young, middle age or old.

The one control that we do have is
To live in harmony with loved ones.
To say I Love you many times so that your loved ones will
Be with you when the time comes.

Ever wonder how you will go?

I Am Here for You

As we idled up the pathway to go into our church
I had already started to ask God for help as my dad needed Divine healing
Doctors told us that there wasn't anything else they could medically do for dad
He was paralyzed, not responsive, and had absolutely no physical feeling

It seems like the doctor's words ignited my need to speak and pray to God
And thus the trip to go to the nearest church, visit with God and to pray
But as we meandered on the pathway leading to go inside the church
Halfway there sat a very deformed man asking for alms, sat there along the way

I grabbed my family, left the pathway, and went around this man
We walked on the grass and eventually made our way back on the path
I looked back to see if this person was still there and felt relieved that we got by
It was a very hot day, and I wondered how long could he sit there, how long could he last

I made my way to the altar to pray and ask God for His help and was taken aback
He spoke to me and said, "Why should I help you when you avoided Me?"

I quickly ran out of the church to see if the deformed man was still there

And to my relief, he was the only one of many there that I could plainly see

I walked up to this man and gave him what little money I had and shook his hand

I looked him in the eye to see if God would wink at me and let me know that He forgave me

I now know that He tested my faith and wanted to see how I would react

Now I know what He meant when He said—they have eyes but do not see

This person even if he was not sent by God to test my faith and Christianity

Is a person of God and one that we the more fortunate should seek and help as best we can

For even as Jesus touched and healed the lepers and others that needed His help

We need to be sincere in helping our Christian brothers and sisters period and amen

I left this man and went back into the church and finished my praying at His altar

Truly felt at ease as I prayed and felt assured that I had passed the test that He had sent

Went back to the hospital to see my dad and found the doctors bewildered and confused

I knew that He had heard my plea for help, I knew the church visit was time very well spent

Through the grace of God and only through His helping and healing hands

Can I honestly say that my dad lived 20 more years after the doctors gave up on him

His paralysis left him and he little by little improved until he was
    dismissed
Walked out of the hospital, was able to feed himself, whistle and even
    sing

You see God does listen to prayer, and He does test us every now and
    then
We just have to see beyond the unfavorable and always trust in His
    way
We have to learn to be humble, obedient, and to serve those less
    fortunate than us
To give thanks for His Blessings, forgiveness, guidance, and love each
    and every day

My God please help me, know You half as much as you know me!

I'll Stay Here

Was it a dream
Walking among angels felt so real
Millions of angels greeting me
Unbelievable yet so surreal

I was shown my room
In that wonderful and huge home
All the beautiful flowers & music
I even got a glimpse of the King on His throne

I was alive again and all my pain was gone
I was walking and running and had no fear
Such a marvelous place to be
Made up my mind that I would stay here

No more jealousy, envy, or hate
No more medicines, pain, or sickness
No more worries, bills, or stress
No more body aches and no more weakness

I am coming home to a place chosen for me
I go content and totally without fear
My room is beautiful and full of bliss
I will wait here for you—"I'll stay here"

It Was an Honor

Today, I woke up after my "wake up call" alarm sounded. Got up from bed and went through the daily ritual that humans go through prior to heading for work. Only this morning, I felt different. Seemed like I had a premonition that today would be different, but not being able to foresee the future I did not know what was going to happen.

Arrived at work and went into my office to commence my workday. Today, I was to chart our company's sales progress and create a graphic presentation to show that detail. By the way, my name is Stanmor, and I take great pride in my work output. I have a phobia and that phobia is that I check data for accuracy not once, not twice, but three times. When I present data, it is very accurate and factual.

I was totally involved with my current task and had no idea that someone had entered my office until my boss said, "Good morning, Stanmor." After the usual and customary greetings were said and done, my boss told me that he'd like to speak with me in his office. Of course, he said he'd like that if I could free up some time. I advised my boss that my initial draft was complete and that I had not commenced the customary checks on my work before the final product so that now was a good time.

I followed my boss to his office and my thought went to my early morning premonition. Something was going to happen today, was this it? Was I going to get fired, laid off, or pulled from the current project team? I guess you can tell I was worried to a very stressful extent.

I was still very nervous once inside the office of my boss and was seated across from his desk. He started asking me the usual questions . . . how was I doing? How is work? How is project team moving? Did I have any concerns? These questions did not help me or ease my nervousness, but only made matters worse. Why does he not go straight to the issue at hand?

My last question was answered to my gratitude and great personal satisfaction. Boss said he was extremely gratified about my work ethics and notably my attention to detail. Went on to present me with a very substantial pay raise. Wow! Talk about a great and positive premonition! Before I left his office, he told me I was doing a very good job!

Thanked my boss for noticing and rewarding me with this pay compensation increase and went back to my office to finish my presentation. I was elated. My chest was puffed outward, and my head was held high. I was on cloud nine. Happy is not a descriptive adjective of how I felt.

At lunchtime, I had decided to go eat lunch at a very exclusive and expensive restaurant that was just blocks away from work. I could walk there and for the very first time eat there. I had never been inside this restaurant as I had heard that their meals were beyond delicious but priced super high.

Today would be different as I was celebrating my good fortune in relation to my superb pay increase. Today would be a day to remember as I was escorted to a seating place and commenced to view the menu.

I ordered a big steak and baked potato and was appalled at price, but again, today, I was splurging and was letting my budget guard down. I could already savor the medium well done steak I had ordered. I was very wishful that this steak would be worth the price I had to pay, but kept remembering that this restaurant was highly recommended for their steaks and other food dishes.

I was sipping my glass of tea when I noticed a disheveled and unkempt man standing outside the main door opening into the restaurant. Man had an overcoat on even though it was unbearably hot outside. I also noticed the restaurant manager or owner swiftly heading toward entrance to potentially confront the person. Once outside, I noticed the restaurant manager/owner waving his arm and motioning for this person to leave the premises. The poor unfortunate soul would not even look at the person telling him to leave or else he'd call police and have him escorted away.

I do not know why I did what I did, but I left my table and proceeded to go outside with these two individuals. Once outside, I asked what the problem was, and the restaurant manager/owner advised me that this person was not welcomed inside his restaurant. I asked the restaurant manager/owner to have my food brought outside as we, the homeless person and I, were going to eat outside on the stairs leading into the restaurant. I also stated that if he would be kind enough to bring me a hamburger and fries along with my steak and potato lunch.

I do not know what or how this happened, but before the restaurant manger/owner had a chance to object to my proposal to eat outside, there was a string of restaurant patrons that had joined us and also voiced their request to eat outside with this poor soul. Wow, talk about power in numbers. Before we knew it, there were more patrons seated outside on stairway than inside restaurant.

I do not know how this event happened, but all the food all of us had ordered was brought out to us at the same time by numerous, numerous waiters. I advised the waiter serving us that the hamburger and fries were for me, and that the steak and potato was for my friend. No sooner had all received their respective order when we heard our poor Christian brother begin a verbal and loud prayer of thanks. To this day, I recollect his fervent prayer, which went like this, "Thank you, Jesus, for this meal which you have allowed us to share from thy unending bounty. Thank you for your many blessings, for life, and especially for kind and friendly people that I have crossed path with today. Thank you for all you do for me, but now I want to ask that you bless all gathered here as much as you have blessed me. In Jesus name, amen!"

At the end of this prayer, I had to look away and hoped no one noticed my eyes full of tears, but as I looked at the rest of those assembled, I noticed that there were no dry eyes on this beautiful and marvelous group. I felt at ease and proud that I had such a caring and sentimental heart.

Today, so far, had been full of pleasant surprises but we, or *He*, were not done yet. The restaurant manager/owner came outside and notified all that were gathered there that a man inside restaurant had paid for all our food. I asked who this kind Christian man was, and the restaurant owner/manager pointed to a man that was giving me a thumbs up. Lord and behold, this man was the same man that hours before had rewarded me with a very healthy pay raise. That man was my boss.

Prior to leaving the restaurant steps, we all pitched in what money we had saved on our meals and presented that money to this humble person, and each one—one by one—thanked the man for his blessing and for allowing them to dine with him. We all felt good about what we had done and had absolutely no regrets whatsoever.

On my way back to work, I still had thoughts about that early morning premonition and thought that my day was done. What else could go positively good for me today? No sooner had I asked that inward question when it seemed like I had a spiritual force walking with me, patting me on my back and saying, "I am proud of you, real good job!"

Kid Utopia

It's ironic how kids can get along and play alongside each other day in and day out.
Their language may be a barrier but very seldom hinders their kinship
Kids have a language all of their own and sometimes play without saying a word.
They bind on the playground and sometimes commence a lasting friendship

Ever notice how kids have a tendency to share their toys without a complaint.
Share their toys with others no matter if the others are of a different color or race.
They speak to each other often even though the others may not understand
You can see the respect just by seeing that they give each other plenty of space

There is no prejudice or ill feelings because the kids do not look like one another.
There is no concept of being inferior or superior in any of the kids' mind
There is only tranquility, friendship, peace, happiness, and joy on their mind
I guess that is the driving force, this positive attitude that makes them bind

Guess we should all go to our local playgrounds and parks
Maybe we'll get lucky to see kids of all colors playing alongside each other.

And just maybe we'll feel the respect and friendship being displayed
Kids taking care of each other just as if they were truly blood brothers

Sometimes some of these kids grow up and forget their playful youth
Forget that they played alongside kids of another race or color
Ignore the fact that some of these kids were truly great kids and
    friends
And that back then race or color was not an issue—was definitely
    not a bother

Unfortunately, we tend to grow and sometimes emulate what we see
    and hear at home.
Take this factor, and use it to guide us through life and the friends
    we choose
Not questioning or remembering that some of the childhood friends
    were not of our race.
Not being concerned about past friendships that we will ultimately
    and forever lose

Why must we grow up and lose all power and will to be with others
    at play or at work?
Why can't we just see all others as simply being human beings with
    a caring heart?
Why must some people always feel like they are far more superior
    than others?
Why do ill feelings continue to exist and where and when did this
    malevolence start?

I am glad and proud to say and live my life alongside others not of
    my color or race
I respect their individuality whether they live in mansions or a house
    made out of sod.
I treasure their input and value their worth both on the playground
    and at work
I ask for forgiveness for any ill feelings toward my friends is my prayer
    to my God

You see, I've learned the lesson of life and plan to live my life as Jesus
would.
Jesus has no ill feelings to anyone and welcomes all that come to Him
He does not look at what you have or do not have or how rich or
poor you are.
He values the fact that you came to Him regardless of the color of
your skin

So I've made up my mind and will forever remain a kid at heart
I'll always remember that language or color will never block the path
to friendship.
I'll ask Jesus for His divine grace and guidance as He fills me with
wisdom and understanding.
I'll ask Jesus to inspire me to learn their language and ways to truly
and forever bind our kinship!

Unfortunately not all think like I do during our troubling era or
time;
But just think—what would today's world be like if we were all blind?
Food for thought or food to ponder . . .
What color is your God? Ever wonder?

Life

As I followed the running water in the creek
I came to a place where the creek split into multiple brooks
I couldn't help but wonder which brook I needed to follow
I cannot explain why the one on the right is the one I took.

I followed this brook with all its bends and turns.
Sometimes the water would be rushing by and other times it was
    slow.
Often the brook would take a very quick turn like it was going back
    to the creek
But then it would turn and turn again as if it didn't know which way
    to go

I kept on following this brook not really knowing where it would
    lead.
I kept looking as far as I could to see if I could see the end.
But the brook kept on going and kept on turning and churning
And I kept on following hoping the end would be just around the
    bend

I noticed as I followed the brook that sometimes the water was fairly
    deep.
But then as if by choice the brook would again turn real shallow.
I also noticed that the brook bed in some places was rocky and full
    of debris.
And sometimes the bed was sandy and clean making it easier to
    follow

I kept on following the brook not really understanding why.

And I was about to stop following the brook and give up on finding the end.

It seemed as if the brook knew my thoughts of not following it anymore.

As a little bit farther it rejoined the creek just around a sharp bend.

Following a creek that breaks out into many, many brooks.

Is no different than life as there are many paths we can take.

We could stay on the main and straight road, but notice that it is seldom traveled.

We take path well traveled only to eventually realize we have made a drastic mistake.

We venture back to where we began or to our initial starting point.

And really look at all the paths right there in front of us and still are confused.

Again we scrutinize the straight, main, and narrow road and contemplate going this way.

But again our inclination leads us to follow a path that shows it is heavily used.

Path we follow is riddled with all kinds of attractions and with lots of opportunities

Path is overcrowded and it seems like you are being pushed to go in crowd's direction

Sometimes the crowd slows down to take in the sights and relish the experience.

Other times the crowd is raucous and anxious to see the next temptation.

The path we have chosen is not straight at all as it keeps turning as if on purpose.

Sometimes the path is lit and more often the path is so dark that you cannot see.

But one constant is that the overbearing crowd keeps on going raucously forward.

But I can't help but wonder, "Why am I here, what's to happen to me?"

I finally reach my senses and fight my way back to where it all began.

I, again, ponder which way I should go or which path I should now take.

After much deliberation while looking at all the paths that showed heavy use.

I decide to take the straight, narrow path hoping this is not another mistake

No sooner do I get on this path that I notice very few travelers.

Another aspect is that the deafening noise of the crowd is not evident

Travelers stop and admire the scenery and are having a joyous time.

Tranquility and caring attitude from the few travelers is quite prevalent

As we go forth we see all kinds of godly attractions that are filled with travelers.

Soft and angelic music is amplified to the travelers as they gather to worship.

Travelers from all kinds of places and religions are joined as one.

True camaraderie exemplified, true meaning of Christian kinship

Having been on the paths that lead to nowhere and had no real true value.

I am finally convinced that I have found the righteous path we all should seek.

I am firmly confident and gratified that I left the paths well traveled.

Left the raucous crowd and fell in pace with the few and humble meek

So you see in life there are numerous paths, which we can follow.
Only one path is straight and narrow but others are full of twists and
    bends.
On only one path will you constantly see and hear about righteousness.
While on the other paths you will travel without achieving a true
    Christian end

I made up my choice and came back to where I always belonged.
How long will it take you to also come back to the righteous path,
    how long?

Moving On

Another day has come and gone
And I still miss you so
I try to think of all the reasons
On why you had to go

I get up on that stage each night
And sing my country songs
But my eyes get cloudy and teary
Just knowing that you're gone

I see all the women there, as I can't keep but notice
I see all the brunettes, redheads, and blondes
But since you've gone I feel so lonely
And it's hard for me to have some fun

Those cheating country songs I sing
Do not reflect our time together
I'd like to sing more sentimental songs
Where we are together forever

It's almost time for me to get on stage
And I'll drawl out my country songs
Hoping I see you in the crowd
But knowing well that you are gone

I guess it's time for me to move on
And leave my pain behind and have some fun
Hopefully I'll meet someone that reminds me of you
Whether she be brunette, redhead, or blonde

My Companion, My Shadow

Living out the country and my parents being poor did not allow us to have store bought toys
Neighbors were too far so I spent a lot of my time running after rabbits in the meadow
I had a lot of free time after all my chores were completed on my dad's little ranch
Free time was mostly spent running by the creek or chasing my illusive and cowardly shadow

My shadow was very unpredictable and never, never stayed in one place for too long
At times, it would be seen in front of me and then later on it would be behind me
It even tried to scare me by getting real big and scary and was a lot bigger than me
But my shadow was a coward because it stayed below every time I climbed a tree

Sometimes my shadow would try to be smart and stay to the right or left of me
And really tried to outsmart me at times by being nowhere to be found
But I knew my shadow pretty well and could almost tell where it would be
I even knew it would not jump into the creek with me for fear that it would drown

At night you could always tell my shadow was not too mean or not at all too brave

It always reached the door first and always went in before I ever
  stepped inside
And even though my shadow always entered the house before I ever
  did
I never saw my shadow inside the house, I think the scary cat would
  always hide

By common reasoning I had finally reached a well thought out
  conclusion
My shadow was quite illusive, but my shadow would get hurt and
  would always cry
I remember one day my shadow was in front of me and was really,
  really big
I remember falling on top of my shadow and saw it cry, I promise
  this is no lie

My shadow cried so much that I could see its hands and arms move
  to cover its eyes
I could see it rolling in pain and heard it let out loud groans as it
  moved in a lot of pain
The shadow's eyes had gotten my eyes soaking wet with all the tears
  and then I felt the pain
I finally admitted that the illusive and cowardly shadow and I were
  one and the very same!

Once I reached this conclusion, it was not hard for me to change my
  mind
I continue to spend a lot of time chasing and running after rabbits
  in the meadow
My attitude toward my shadow has changed quite a bit as my shadow
  and I are one
We are both strong, fearless, brave, seldom cry, and I love being with
  my companion, my shadow

One More Chance

As a youngster, I was always pushing the limit
Always getting in trouble by not listening and adhering to rules
And once I was being disciplined I would cry and
Could not understand why my parents were angry and cruel
And I would plead—please give me one more chance!

In grade school I was always horsing around and had my fun
But when the teacher scolded me and applied some discipline
I would try to argue and change the teacher's mind
But at the end I would try to understand the teacher's reason
And I would plead—please give me one more chance!

So as I grew and got involved in sports
I still had not learned how to act
When coach got upset with me and applied his discipline
At two of our games on the bench I sat
And I would plead—please give me one more chance

My next step in life was High School and things were unchanged
I was still getting in trouble and still believe I was set-up
I was speaking to one of my girlfriend's enemies and once she saw us
She told me that I should have known better and that it was time to
    break up
And I would plead—please give me one more chance!

College here I come and again the world was not stopping for me
I still was very insecure and definitely very immature
I had missed several assignments and had marginal grades

Professor told me my incompetence would make me fail for sure
And I would plead—please give me one more chance!

The job market was calling and I was lucky enough to get a job
But my priorities were all over the place and not properly aligned
My boss called me in and reprimanded me and let me know where
    I stood
Said that I would not get a raise and another project to me he would
    not assign
And I would plead—please give me one more chance!

Years have come and gone and I have left my friends behind
Retirement is mine and I am enjoying life and spending money
My wife is pretty upset with me because of my new life style
Here is what she said—"if you do not change I am leaving you honey"
And I would plead—please give me one more chance!

Old age crept in, and I hardly noticed until
The day I got real sick and felt really, really bad
I moped around and did not know what to do
I showed my anger, fear, despair and was really sad
But I turned to God and this was my plea—please give me one more
    chance

Prayer from Patient

Today, I prayed for you . . .
I asked Jesus to strengthen you and to give you the skill, knowledge, and tools to perform needed medical procedure.
I asked Jesus to guide your hands and to take control of your mind so that you may stay in control and help me while in your care.
I asked Jesus to help you help me!
I asked Jesus to give me needed strength to go thru medical procedure.
I also asked Jesus for a speedy and uneventful recovery.
I thanked Jesus for His help and for sending a caring doctor to perform my medical procedure.
Today, I prayed for both of us!

Prayer from Doctor
Today, I prayed for you . . .
I asked Jesus to strengthen you and to keep you positive and healthy during medical procedure.
I asked Jesus to give me needed skill, knowledge, and tools to properly perform needed medical procedure.
I asked Jesus to come and stay with me during medical process.
I asked Jesus to help me help you!
I asked Jesus for his guidance.
I asked Jesus to help you to quickly get healthy and strong after medical procedure.
I thanked Jesus for listening to my prayer.
Today, I prayed for both of us!

Prayer Times Two

Imagine for a minute that you were allowed to visit with Jesus
How would you act and much more what would you say?
Would you be over-whelmed by His presence?
Would you carry a conversation or would you just Pray?

Here is what I believe Jesus would say:
Why won't you listen to Me?
Why won't you help Me?
Why do you turn your back on Me?
Why don't you care for Me?
Why do you let others hurt Me?
Say bad things about Me?
Why do you deny Me?
Why won't you protect Me?
Fight for Me?
Defend Me?
Heal My wounds?
Take My cause to the Father?
Why don't you help Me prosper?
Why don't you help My family?
My loved ones? Why do I have to suffer?
Why can't I have you beside Me all the time?
Why can't you see the suffering?
Why have you given up on Me?
Why do you not trust Me to do your will?
More importantly why don't you love Me as I love you?
Keep in mind that this is what Jesus would ask of each one of us, and
    I am sure that we have prayed/asked Jesus for more than one of
    the questions listed above.

Thus, you can see that Jesus has heard our plea and felt our suffering
And through it all He has given us much more . . .
He has given us His love.
Remember next time we pray . . . are we asking for something that
    Jesus has also asked from us?
Are we listening?
Are we using our eyes to see?
Our ears to hear?
Our hearts to lead us to Him?
Why won't you let Him into your heart?

Prayer to Thee

As I lay on my hospital bed unable to do much
I'm totally powerless of the sickness in control of me
I cannot turn to family, friend or any man
I cry out to God—I cry for help from Thee

I look for signs that He has heard my plea or prayer
It seems that He is too busy to help or have pity on me
But just like the widowed woman with the earthly unruly judge
I persistently cry out to God—I cry for help from Thee

Just as I finished asking God for His help
The door to my room opened and the doctor walked into the room
Doctor said that they would run all kinds of tests on me
Diagnose my sickness and get me back to feeling well soon

I closely looked at this doctor that was sent to help me
I wanted to see the doctor's halo or even a glimpse of the doctor's
    angel wings
Doctor was real cautious about what was said or done
Said I should keep on praying—see what tomorrow brings

My doctor consulted with other doctors after some tests were run
Prescribed some medication, which the doctor said would help me
    get well soon
Little by little, I felt like I was getting healthier and much more alert
Doctor always asked—do you have any questions before I leave the
    room?

It's ironic how life has a tendency to humble even the strongest
You go from one extreme to the other without a thing you can do
Next thing you know you are being transported to a hospital
Hospital nurses and doctors trying to take care of you

It's also weird how you think of all that is suddenly happening to you
All kinds of crazy thoughts infiltrate your head
You think of your life and your family and what's to become of them
Unpleasant thoughts as you lay on a stiff hospital bed

But turning to prayer and to God for His help
Is much more agreeable than thinking bad thoughts
Thinking real positive and staying in control
Reading the bible—reading His words

God has a way of answering your prayers
Even though He knows we have not stayed the course
Sends His angels to all who ask for help
Angels in the form of a doctor or a very special nurse

Now I know and vouch that God does hear our plea
Hears all that cry out—God have pity and mercy on me
Sends His best doctors and nurses to cure our disease
Speaks softly to us—I will protect, love, and cure thee

In my sickness I cried out to Thee
You heard my plea and set out to rescue me
My gratitude, my love, and my pledge of loyalty forever
Along with my life that as long as I live belongs to Thee

In my time of wellness, I will honor and forever thank Thee
Because in my time of distress, You rushed to cure and help me

Remember Me

I do not know how I got here nor do I remember why
Sporadically I do understand that I was not always like this
I tend to remember the good times we had and some of the places we've been
Occasionally recollect the joyous family ties, which were always full of bliss

I may look at you and know and feel your anguish and pain
And even though my bewildered look may cause you some confusion
Know that my heart still knows who you are and will forever until the end
Please forgive me for what I have become—a distant illusion

I see you and also know when you come by to see me and when you stay away
And even though I may not show my emotion, I truly love the time we spend together
Your warm and loving embrace and kind words positively infiltrate my body and soul
I long for the good old days when we were extremely loving and happy together

Yet sometimes I see your bewildered look and notice your posture and teary eyes
Was it something I said or failed to say to cause you to act like this?
Maybe it was my inability to focus and carry a sound and essential conversation
I do not understand sometimes but know that my family I profoundly miss

It used to be that the years would pass us by and our inclination was
to forget

But now the years have evolved into days if not into hours and
minutes

I wish I knew and understood what is becoming of me and what is
really happening

But at night, I have sweet dreams of our bond, a wonderful dream
with you and me in it

I wish and pray that I would be a lot more forthright and recollect a
lot more

But again, understand that I am puzzled by what is transpiring within
my body and mind

I want so badly to hold you and call you by your name and positively
reassure you

But what ails me is traumatic and uncontrollable and definitely not
very kind

I want you to look at me and understand this very important and
essential fact

The person you see is the person that cared and loved you and helped
build our family tree

So please forgive my inaptitude to understand and to really show my
love

But please look closely—I am in this body—please be patient and
always remember me!

Remember me saying—I love you!

Sound Familiar?

Father to son/daughter . . . while you live under my roof, you will abide by the following rules:

1. Obey/respect your mother at all times
2. Do not talk back to me or your mom
3. Do not fight with your brother/sister
4. Do not use curse words in this house
5. Be polite to older people
6. Do not drink/smoke while living here
7. Do not do or be near anyone that uses drugs
8. Do not drive car too fast . . . stay below speed limit
9. Be home by or before curfew
10. Do not take/keep anything that is not yours

Son/daughter, meet with parents to discuss rules and propose the following rule changes:

1. Obey mother when she is right
2. Won't talk back unless we are in the right
3. Will only fight if my space is violated
4. Will try to minimize curse words used
5. I will respect older people by avoiding them
6. Will only drink/smoke as needed to be liked by friends
7. Will look the other way when friends use drugs
8. Will only drive fast when running late
9. Will call to get curfew extended
10. Will give item(s) back when asked for

Does the above sound familiar?

Makes you wonder what we would propose for the ten rules/commandments that our Father handed down to us, even though no one has met with the Father to propose changes. *His* Ten Commandments are set in stone, but not engraved in all *his* children's hearts.

Why should we be surprised when our rules are not followed? Imagine the pain our God has to go through every day because we cannot follow rules.

Swing

Many years ago as I sat on a park swing
My mind wandered off and made a correlation between a swing and life
Logic was that life, much like a swing has its ups and downs
Sometimes moving fast, then slow, causing anxiety and sometimes fright

On the way upward, we feel exhilarated and in total control
We feel like we have mastered our destiny and totally at our best
We envision that we have truly achieved our goal of having all we want
We are in utmost denial that this happiness will forever last

But then much like a swing we start the downward sweep
Life has a way of bringing you back down to earth and to the present day
Tragically, a loved one lost the battle of life or the stock market fell apart
These are life's lessons or trials and tribulations sent our way

At times, we just sit and let our mind conjure up reasons or excuses
Of why our life has stalled and seems like it is going nowhere
We tend to be judgmental and our negative persona takes control
Telling us to be content with what we have by saying—Life is not fair

For it does not matter if your swing is idle or how fast or high your swing may go
Or how high up the corporate ladder you reach and successfully attain

And it does not matter how fast or crooked your downward swing
    may feel
Keep in mind that He pushes the unfortunate and successful—treats
    all the same

If only we could learn the simple lesson I am trying to convey
And that is that God will push and pull you if you just let Him lead
    the way
Only thing that He may seek is that we acknowledge His presence in
    our ups and downs
That we thank Him for never leaving us and being with us on that
    swing day after day

So next time you go by a park and see a person on a swing or maybe
    just sitting there
Imagine that this person is not alone no matter if the swing is idle,
    going down or up
You can hear Him whispering in the successful person's ear, keep
    being who you are
And to the desolate person you can hear Him say, keep fighting, push
    forward, and don't stop

How beautiful is our God that he treats all the same and knows each
    one of us by name
Some He rewards with a superb mind and others with a beautiful
    voice to sing
But through it all, we must give Him thanks for all He does for us
Whether it be on an idle, moving upward, or spiraling downward in
    life or on a swing!

Special Pennies

I was pretty gullible as a young man
    My dad gave me two pennies and told me to save them as long
    as I can
My dad said that the pennies were very special
Said one penny was a Lincoln and the other penny was an Abraham
I held onto these pennies as much as I did to my dad's words
Being special pennies, I did not show these to anyone not even to
    my mom
I clutched these pennies and protected them as best I could
Knowing full well that like my two pennies there were not any to be
    found—none
My youthful years turned into my terrible and rebellious teen years
I now knew my dad had fibbed a little when he said that the two
    pennies were special
But I still remember the gleam in my dad's eyes when he handed
    these pennies to me
I wish he were still here to see my other valuables and my two special
    pennies in my satchel

I guess my dad taught me a very special lesson and one that I will
    relay to my sons
It's not the size or value of the gift, but what we say upon giving
    something of value
It's the lesson of accepting and protecting and holding onto some-
    thing of importance
It's in lovingly giving and never saying the words that inspired the
    gift—I love you

My two pennies are still with me and will forever until it's time for
    me to go
I see them and touch them and always think of my hero and try not
    to cry as best I can
I can still see my dad standing tall with a slight grin on his face and
    saying those words
These pennies are special as one is a Lincoln and one is an Abraham

Dad, I know you are up there in heaven and your grin is now a big
    smile
I want to say I thank you for being my dad, which I know you already
    knew
And to show you how much I miss you, love you, and constantly
    think of you
When its time for me to go, I've got two special pennies I'll be hand-
    ing back to you

Have You Seen God?

There once was a very learned man that wanted some answers
He wanted to know if God existed and if anyone had actually seen God
He wandered off his house one day and commenced to find the answer to his concern
But everywhere he looked and thought God would be, He was not

He went so far to ask a man that looked like he was a very prominent man
Asked the man if he knew God and more importantly if he had seen God?
The man was startled as no one had ever asked him so bluntly about God
He said to your question about seeing God the answer is no I have not

The man searching for answers came upon an elderly lady and approached her to ask
Do you know God and more importantly have you ever seen God?
Man thought this woman, being up in her age, surely would give some good advise
But just like the man before the elderly woman said—the answer is no I have not

The man then approached a young lad riding his bike down the street
Asked the young lad if he knew God and more importantly if he had seen God?
The young lad was bewildered and didn't know what to say but gave him his answer
Reiterated what he had heard from the other two—the answer is no I have not

He kept on mulling this question in his head and was letting his
   mind wander

Approached a young woman and asked her if she knew God or had
   seen God?

The young lady didn't know what to say and thought that maybe this
   was a joke

She went along trying not to laugh and answered—the answer is no
   I have not

So far, he had asked four different persons and not one was very
   helpful

Went into church and asked the priest, "Do you know God and have
   you seen God?"

Priest went on to say, "God is everywhere, and you'll find Him when
   He wants you to"

But the answer to your question about seeing Him—the answer is
   no I have not

The learned man had no where else to turn and yet he had not yet
   gotten his answer

He knew God existed as all things are His creation and He teaches
   about kindness and love

While sitting at a park bench, mulling what his next step would be
   and where he would go

He noticed a butterfly descended and landed on his shoulder and on
   the other shoulder a dove

He kept looking at the butterfly and marveled at the beautiful colors
   on the butterfly

But was also deeply impressed by the calmness and beauty of the
   cooing dove

Man thought that this cannot be happening as this occurrence is not
   supposed to happen

But then he thought—maybe this is a sign from His Holy Angels or
   directly from God

God was showing me that He does exist and can be seen whenever
one looks

Will be in the form of man, elderly woman, young boy, young
woman, priest, butterfly, or dove

God will always be there when we seek Him and ask for His help and
is never far away

Constantly walking beside us or watching over each one of us from
His throne up above

You see, when I went looking for God, I went looking and asking the
strong and well off

I should have been looking for God among the weak, old, homeless
and meek

I should have known He would be humble like the butterfly and the
dove

If I had looked among the frail, sick and those that are lost—amongst
them—God I would meet

I finally relaxed as God had once again convinced me that He is in
total control

Spoke to me thru the butterfly and dove and said—be kind, consid-
erate, and loving in all you do

Be compassionate and help all those that truly need help and encour-
age others to do the same

Keep on walking in My steps and rest assured I will always be right
beside you!

Do what I tell you and again you can rest assured that I will always
be by your side

Keep on being a true Christian, and you will always have my Blessings
and have Me near

And if you look close enough, you will probably say I know God and
have seen Him

Look closely at the people you help, for no one knows how, when,
and where I will appear!

It Wasn't Supposed to
End this Way

As a young, little boy I had feelings for you that I could not explain
I watched you as your family moved into the house next door
I kept staring at you not really understanding why
But I vowed, "This will be my first girlfriend for sure."

Time was kind to both of us as we grew and left our childhood behind
I cannot help but think of the times we played house and you were
    the mom and wife
You made me play daddy and advised me on how to take care of you
    and the house
Told me to act, which was not hard, to think that you were the sole
    purpose for my life

I also recollect all the times we played hide and seek and all the laugh-
    ter we shared
The time spent on the swings as I pushed you to go as high as you
    could
The time we shared drinking coffee or drinks from your play cups
    or plates
I was in heaven just being close to you . . . time was at a stand still,
    time was good

But as all things, we grew and this is where we strayed apart a bit
My feelings for you were still strong, and I missed you so much when
    we were not together

I hated to see you drive off to school or at nighttime when you went
   inside your house
I thought that someday I would tell you how I felt and we'd be
   together forever

I guess it was not very evident of the love I had for you from the very
   first time I saw you
And I guess I was afraid to tell you as I thought that would drive you
   away
But now that you know that I loved you from the very first time and
   will forever more
I apologize for telling you this on your wedding day, but I cannot
   help but think—it was not supposed to end this way

Good luck, my love and, may your life be blessed beyond belief
I'll always remember this wedding day and will never forget this day
I'll always love you, think of you, and will remember you and all the
   good times we had
But, especially, I want you to know—it wasn't supposed to end this
   way!

Mary Lou and Stan

My name is Stan and this is my remarkable story. For years, I would wake up real early in the morning, have my coffee, dress, and venture out to get my daily walking exercise. Not to get too carried away, I would only walk a block or two, depending on how well I felt, around our neighborhood. Today was no exception. I, and my trusted walking stick, were traversing a path that we knew quite well, but today would be the start of a miraculous day. Let me explain.

As mentioned we, my walking stick and I, walked the same route for many years, and we probably could walk it blindfolded. I used a walking stick not as a necessity but used it as a tool to ward off dogs or push sticks off the pathway. It was my security blanket. Now back to my story about why I felt this would turn out to be a miraculous day. As I walked and studied the neighborhood, I noticed that an advertisement had been stapled to a corner telephone pole. My curiosity led me to read this sign, and I was bewildered why I had been drawn to this advertisement about a Rock and Roll dance being held tonight at our local Community House.

Time was set from 8:00 p.m. to 12 midnight. No sense in stating who the band was as I did not know or had ever heard of this particular group. To say I was bewildered is stating it mildly. Why was I captivated by this advertisement, and more importantly why was I contemplating attending this rock and roll noisy event? Was I losing my mind? Was my mind telling me that I could still enjoy loud music, fast movements, psychedelic lights, and constant screaming? Rest assured my body was not in complete accord with my feeble adventurous mind.

My mind won, and again it was not totally dependent on what I sensed my mind was telling me, but also on a unique and unexplainable force that was seeming to steer me into attending this rock and roll fest. I followed my intuition and arrived around 9:00 p.m. at the gathering place. Way before I entered the Community House, I could hear the thunderous, aggravating, and annoying unrhythmic music, and the loud screams that almost drowned the singer and the music. Was I ready for this? Could I survive this night? Why was I here, and better yet, why did I feel that an unseen force was pushing me onward? As imagined, it was extremely loud and annoying to see all these dancers moving in ways that I only imagined I could have at one point in my life.

The flickering and colorful lighting were enough to drive anyone with vertigo into dizzy convulsions, but again, when I turned and as I tried to leave, there was this unseen force pushing me onward. I thought, *Okay, I am game, now what?* Well, no sooner had that thought infiltrated my mind when I got my answer. There across from the dance floor was a table with only one chair and was being illuminated for some strange reason. Keep in mind that the rest of the place had all these on/off colorful lights going but not this particular table. Why? I made my way to see if this table and chair were not taken and wished that if they were not, that some more agile person may not beat me there. I made it without any issues and sat at that table and chair, which now I know was set there through divine intervention. Set there for only me to use. Here comes that constant question, why? Again, it was almost an immediate reply to my question. I looked out at the other side of the dance floor and there she was. Her table was also lit up beyond belief, but not even the luminous light could match or equal the radiant beauty of this woman.

I hate to keep bringing this question up, but why were my table and hers the only ones illuminated? A few songs went by and the raucous crowd kept getting louder and louder, and the only reason I had not left is that I was enthralled by this beautiful, white haired, neatly combed, nicely, and modestly dressed angel that sat across this dance floor. I know she caught me numerous times just staring at her. My not-so-feeble and timid mind kept urging me to walk across the dance floor and ask her to dance with me, but I thought why would someone this beautiful dance with me? To say I was in a quandary is an understatement. Bombs were going off all around me, yet I could not move. Why am I so attracted to this woman, and what if she accepts my offer to dance? Rock and roll? Seriously! My mind eventually won the battle with my body, and I nervously eased up to this very beautiful woman and asked her if she would like to dance. Well, what happened next floored me and convinced me that, not only was she beautiful, but that she was also a very strong woman that, without reservations, stated what was on her mind. Her answer to me was, "What took you so long to ask me to dance?" I noticed that you kept staring at me and I was almost at the point to ask you to dance as I thought you did not have the courage to ask me. By the way, my name is Mary Lou, and what is your name?"

I answered, "My name was Stan," and that she was right. I had been staring at her as I was totally infatuated with her beauty and wondered what two four times past teenagers were doing at a rock and roll dance. I told her I really admired that we both had the same hair stylist that loved to color our hair white. She chuckled and then brought me back to earth and said, "Are we dancing or not?"

Of course, as you can imagine, here I was asking this angel to dance to a rock and roll song that I noticed the majority of dancers on the dance floor were jumping up and down. Here goes, I told her that there is no way we will mimic their dance style, but let's dance like we know how. Let's pretend Ole Blue Eyes is drooling out one of his love songs and just enjoy the moment.

Mary Lou agreed, and we commenced our slow rhythmic dance amongst all the others that were set on killing all the bugs on the dance floor.

I imagine or I actually heard some laughter and some heckling being diverted at us, but I could care less as, right now, I was as close as I could get to heaven. Unbeknown to us, some of the dancers had relinquished the dance floor to us and were applauding this old couple for being courageous enough to go against the grain. As I looked at some of the attendees there, young men and women, I also noticed that some had tears in their eyes. Imagined that they were shedding tears of joy as true love was being displayed right there in front of them. We finished this dance and danced many more and by now we were the main attraction. We were getting complimentary remarks left and right and that truly helped put us at ease.

We were in utopia as now, that I recollect, the music was no longer loud or annoying. The music was divine, which complimented quite fittingly my dance partner. As all good things, time has a way of catching up, and we were advised by the band that this would be our last dance. I asked Mary Lou if she would like to have this last dance and she, this time without putting me in my place, eagerly agreed.

As we danced the final dance of this concert, I kept hoping that the music would never end. I had an angel in my arms and did not want to turn her loose. It happened, the dance ended, and I was now a different man. I asked Mary Lou if I could call her and take her out and get to know her. Told her that of all the things I ever wanted that this request was the grandest of all. I would never ask for anything else in my remaining lifetime again. Mary Lou moved real fast and left our table at a fast pace, but before she did, I noticed the tears in her eyes. Was Mary Lou rejecting me or my offer to get close to her, or was there something else? Again, here comes that strange force that seemed to be lifting me off my chair and instructing me to catch her. I did as my feelings lead me to and did catch up to Mary Lou.

I gently stopped Mary Lou and asked her to tell me, "What's wrong?"

Mary Lou cannot stop crying and keeps looking away from me. Three or four young lads came by and asked Mary Lou, "Is this man bothering you or hurting you?"

Mary Lou finally looked at me and answered, "This wonderful man is hurting me with *love*! I am okay, and we are okay."

She thanked the young men for their concern. Mary Lou becomes Mary Lou again and tells me, "Stan, we have to talk. You see I have had a wonderful time—such a wonderful time that I have never experienced before in my lifetime. You, Stan, are the reason, and I'll always be grateful to you, but, Stan, here comes the worst or best part of our short-lived love story. The doctor told me two months ago that I had two months to live. Told me there is no cure for me, and, Stan, this is my final week of those two months. I do not know what force brought me here or under what circumstance

I read that advertisement about this dance tonight or what driving force guided me here against my logical reasoning. But through it all, our tables, being the only ones lit, and the wonderful time we spent, I now know what heaven will be like, and I thank God for showing me you and what waits for me."

With tears streaming down our faces and before reality had actually and firmly set in, Mary Lou again dashed away from me and headed toward the exit. I cannot explain what happened next, it's been a very long time since I have moved so quickly as I did trying to catch up to Mary Lou.

I, again, gingerly grabbed Mary Lou's arm and stopped her. I told her to listen to me as I also had a story to tell. I told Mary Lou that I also was led to read the dance advertisement, coerced by some divine force to attend this dance, which went against all normal logic for people my age. I also quiver, yet marvel, at why only our tables were lit. "I do not know if you noticed it, but the light was actually on us all the time we were dancing and followed up back to our table. Was that just our imagination, coincidence, or divine intervention? Mary Lou, I think it was divine intervention, and it is through His grace that now I ask for your hand in marriage. I know your time here on earth is limited, but I cannot see myself without you for whatever time He has in place for you. I'd like to share and be part of you during your last minutes, hours, or days, and, together, we can pray for added or borrowed time. Please, Mary Lou, accept my offer to be my bride and wife and that will make me the happiest man on this great green earth."

Mary Lou could not stop crying, but once she had enough wind in her lungs, she answered, "Stan, if I accept your offer, but I do want you to know . . . I hope you have better clothes then those old khaki pants and that pull on faded polo shirt. Do you have better shoes than those old Dr. something shoes? I accept your offer and will try to be all that you think that I am. We will cherish our time together and have no regrets for what ever happens next. Stan, I barely know you, but I love you so much and would have died tonight if I had not seen you again. Thank you for being so agile and catching up to me."

Stan thought, *Wow, Mary Lou is back*! Thank you, God, for getting us past this hurdle. Stan advised Mary Lou that they needed to go see Father Jim who was the local priest at the Catholic Church he routinely attended. Mary Lou cringed and said, "Stan, look at the time, it's almost 1:00 a.m. No normal, old person is up at this time of the day. Can it wait until tomorrow?"

"No, Mary Lou, our time is the most valuable resource we have, and as such, our time is very limited per your earlier confession. Tonight is the night we ask Father Jim to marry us, besides Father Jim is not only my priest, but he is also my friend. I do have his cell phone number, which he gave to me and said that I could call him at any time or for any reason. This visit truly fits his statement. Mary Lou, my future wife, will you accompany me to see Father Jim? He'll want to see you and hear from you that you are willing to take our marriage vows."

Mary Lou excitedly answered, "Yes!"

Stan, as stated above, normally was a very caring and cautious man. Meticulous in his thoughts, actions, and deeds, but tonight he was on a mission.

Tonight, he brought his future bride and himself to Father Jim to set their wedding date. Father Jim was not overly concerned about being pulled out of bed. Normally, priests get calls at all times of the day and night to go give last rites to anyone in need, so their door or telephone line is always open to all. When Father Jim asked the usual questions such as how long we'd known each other and what church Mary Lou attended, had she been baptized, confirmed, and did she believe in God? Mary Lou answered all questions to the best of her ability, but I intervened and told Father Jim our story. I commenced from both of us being lured to read the rock and roll advertisement, the driving unseen force pushing us to attend, the light illuminating only our tables, and us as we danced and finally Mary Lou's confession of being in her final week to live according to her doctor. Father Jim, being a compassionate man and more importantly a symbolic representative of Jesus, told us that under normal circumstances he could not marry us, but that our story was so unique and our union had been blessed from above that he would marry us tomorrow at the 8:30 a.m. mass. Father Jim asked if this was too early for us. I looked at Mary Lou, and she looked at me. We knew we had to accept this time frame, but what were we going to wear? Where could we get customary wedding clothes at this time of the day or before 8:30 a.m. tomorrow.

Mary Lou said she had a beautiful white dress that she rarely used and could wear that tomorrow. Stan said that he also had a very nice dress suit that he hardly ever wore and some nice leather shoes that he seldom used, so the wedding was on for tomorrow at 8:30 a.m. Wedding date went without a hitch. Stan had arranged for a limousine to pick up Mary Lou and him and take them to church. Limousine driver was instructed that this blissful couple wanted to be at church by 8:00 a.m. and not any later. Who wants to be late on their wonderful wedding day? Once mass was over, Mary Lou and Stan were driven to Stan's house where Stan had a surprise waiting for Mary Lou. As per agreement, once Mary Lou reached Stan's main entrance, the limousine driver picked up Mary Lou and carried her inside the house.

Stan followed and winked a big thank you at the driver as he could not have done that in his golden age years. Driver wished Stan and his lovely wife the very best that life could give and felt honored that he had been part of our wedding ceremony. Well, reality has a way of bringing you back to earth rather quickly, and, in some cases, rather crudely and unexpectedly. First thing Mary Lou said once driver had left is that she wanted to inspect the house to see if everything was in order, spotless, and clean. Stan thought, *Mary Lou is back to being her beautiful and wonderful self,* and for that, he thanked God! Mary Lou and Stan spent two wonderful days and nights together. Every night, just before going to sleep, they would crawl into bed, kneeling was out of the question, and Mary Lou would say the following prayer, "God, thank you for the many blessings you have given us and continue to give, thank you for being so caring, loving, and forgiving. Thank you for all you do for us, but, tonight, I ask you dear God that if I do not wake up tomorrow, that you care for this wonderful man beside me. Give him strength to pick up after himself, give him wisdom to know how to keep my house clean, and give him knowledge that I may come back as an angel every now and then to inspect the house. Thank you and good night our God!"

Mary Lou must have had a premonition that this was her last night as sometime during the night, the angels did come for her. She neither cried out or moaned or woke me up to say goodbye, but we knew this was going to happen sooner than later. Stan had no regrets or ill feelings toward our God as he knew He had blessed their lives by bringing them together in Mary Lou's final days. As Stan hugged, kissed, and looked at the beauty of Mary Lou's motionless body, he said his final goodbye and apologized to Mary Lou at the same time.

Stan knew she would have the final say so upon seeing each other again, but here is what Stan whispered in Mary Lou's ear, "My love, I have been trying to get enough nerve to tell you that divine intervention did bring us together as we both had so much in common. Your confession to me was so earth shattering and hit so close to home as I also have been diagnosed with an incurable disease and had been given four months to live. And you know what, this is my final week, if not days. So with that said, I will not say goodbye, my love, but will truly say, I'll see you again real soon!"

Teacher Misery

I 'm in early today and as I sit behind my desk
I can see all my students as if they were here
I can hear me say *Good morning class today is the day*
And at those words my eyes fill up with salty tears

Why did I have to follow this ungrateful profession
When my heart goes out to each and every class?
When all year long we have so much fun
Why do I have to tell some—you did not pass?

It's funny how all last night I wept
And how I prayed that morning would not come
Cause of all the kids that needed more time
Were those in trouble—for them school had just begun

It must be time for me to start with my class
Cynthia and Carlos just said—Good morning, Miss
Oh how I wish our laws were different
So I could love my children with a great big kiss

Good morning John, Mary, Vickie, and Carl
Please go to your desk and please sit down
Joe and Victor, did you leave your manners behind?
Since when do we enter the classroom playing around?

Well, it seems like everyone is here today
So I guess we are very lucky in a way
Cause children the ladder is set pretty high
And for some in this grade it will be your last day

For those that have not made the grades to pass
Please do not think that I was not fair
I am leaving you behind so you will not stumble
Leaving you behind because for you I truly care

Please remember what I have taught and all that you have learned
I'll miss each and everyone of you as we end this school year
I'll look forward to seeing you again as we start another school year
Cause then I'll see you all again and throughout the school year have
  you near

As the children leave and come up to me to thank me for being their
  teacher
I try my best to turn away and hide my joy, pain, misery, and tears
Knowing full well that this scene will be repeated over and over again
As we end another wonderful yet miserable but beautiful school year.

Young One in Schoolroom

Golly, of all the things I could be doing today. Why, by now, I could have caught four or five big fish down by our old fishing hole where me and my daddy always go on a hot, blistering beautiful day like today. I might even decide to play football and knock around my little brother. Or gosh it's been a long, long time since I played baseball. I think that, by now, I have forgotten how to throw a round the table curve as my daddy called it when he was teaching me. You know, I have a BB gun, and, just maybe, I could be shooting some of those darn woodpeckers.

I do not like woodpeckers. Come to think of it, it's been a long time since me and my slingshot, and a couple of special home picked rocks, went busting church windows or hitting caged dogs. I can hit those dogs pretty good. I remember last year when we went fishing—me and my dad—and I fell in the water. I had been clowning around when I fell. Well, being that, I had already been told to settle down. I was left to fight for my life in the water for what seemed like hours and hours. All I remember is my daddy grabbing me by the shirt collar and almost draining me of what little life I had left. It was so funny! Oops—I mustn't laugh here. Remember last year, I was playing like I was the rifleman, and I shot a woodpecker.

Oh, how I hate those darn birds. Well, I kept shooting at this particular woodpecker for four or five blocks when, finally, it quit ducking my BB shot. Down it came off the tree. I ran over to pick it up and strangle it, but the darn bird was still alive and it bit my hand. My hand still hurts now that I think about that. Ouch! Oops, hope nobody heard me. You know, for being a preacher, Mr. Jones almost killed me with the spanking he gave me. My seat was numb for a very long time with that punishment he gave me for no reason at all.

Why, I remember Bully Parks had broken three more church windows while a church meeting was going on. Billy busted three more windows than I did. Today, I still do not think Preacher Jones was fair when I only busted ten church windows during Sunday morning worship. I can still see those people coming out of church running after me and shouting for me to stop. I didn't stop, but I guess Preacher Jones knew who I was as he found me Sunday afternoon. Ooh, how my seat hurts just thinking of that. I'd better stand up. Oh no, what will I do now? I know, "Can I please go to the restroom?" Ah, freedom at last. I think I'll go into the girl's restroom and scare a couple. I ain't done that in a long time.

Then, after that, I'll catch a lizard or two and give them to Nancy. She's the teacher's pet. I do not like her cause she looks like a woodpecker. Maybe I'll catch a spider and place it on Mrs. Rosas, oops, Mrs. Rojas' desk. I wonder what she will do. I better get out of the girl's bathroom before some darn teacher comes along and ruins everything. I guess I'd better get back to class. I just cannot wait to hear the stories Mrs. Rojas said she was going to say today.

As the boy sits at his desk, the school bell rings signaling dismissal time. Schools out for today. Little boy on the way out tells Mrs. Rojas, "You know, I learned a lot today. Moral: ironically, this charade of dreams is evident in every child going to school. I remember when I did it. Do you?"

Take Me

Sitting at church looking up and thinking of you
    Laughing inwardly but with teary eyes
    As always I felt you close by and prayed the same prayer
You always knew I was weak and could not say goodbye
I prayed take me, take me, please take me

The time we shared was divine . . . we were a modern Romeo and
        Juliet
The love we shared was unique and one of a kind
The moments we shared were blessed beyond belief
The tears still flow and blind my eyes
And I still pray take me, take me, please take me

My prayer is simple and comes straight from my heart
My love for you grows with each passing day
But it's been 20 years since I said goodbye
But it seems like yesterday when I prayed
Take me, take me, please take me

You were dealt a life with complications
But I never saw you different nor saw you complain
You loved me and daily gave thanks for our Blessings
You always saw and had sunshine despite the thunder and rain
And that is why I prayed take me, take me, please take me

The day finally arrived when I breathed my last
My last wish was to have our ashes combined together
To spread our ashes out in the ocean

That way we would be together forever
People swear that as our ashes were spread that they heard
Take us, take us, please take us!

The Difference

Vivacious, aggressive, agile, and daring
Only some of the traits that identified my personality
Alluring, admirable, humorous, and outgoing
Described my being in all reality

Athletic, aloof, talented, and gifted
Were adjectives that described God's gift to me
Sharp witted, problem solver, and willing to help others
By explaining the formula so that they could see

Hyper, involved, always volunteered, and dedicated
Admirable traits possessed by only a few
Timely, accurate, punctual, and always present
Focused and always willing to answer questions that few knew

Team member, team captain, and involved in scholastic activities
Encouraged others to join school clubs
Never looked for glory or to get all the praise
Which was one way of getting others to think outside the box

Early riser, self motivated, always thinking on ways to improve
Traits that I always took to work
People person, friendly, and easy to talk to
Going against the grain may be my only quirk

Always on time and never left work early
Willing to help even though our workday was through
Talented, dependable, reliable, and trustworthy
Pretty descriptive of those that knew

Always completed assignments on time
Never complained about workload or demands
Kept on being positive and kept stride with goals
Always asked for help as a favor and not a command

But, you see, things that were are no longer there
The way my mind worked is a thing of the past
The simple things we did in our youth and up to middle age
Are simply gone with time and did not last

Today, I'd like to challenge someone my own age to a foot race
Not to get carried away we would set the distance at 20 yards
Or even a game of darts that we must throw
And warn those around us to watch out for errand darts

I'd like to be able to tie my shoes with ease as I used to do
And get rid of all my shoes that have Velcro straps
To be able to see objects/street signs far and near
Without eyeglasses to read newspaper or city maps

To be able to bend over without a worry or fear of falling
I'd like to sit and stand as quick as I used to in my youth
To remember things/happenings both present or past
To remember my wife's name—is it Betty, Sue, or Ruth?

A blessing would be to control all the shaking my body does
To be able to kneel and send prayer to our Lord above
To be able to feel pain and express my thought without a doubt
To control my anger and express to those close to me my love

To get rid of all the meds I have to take daily
To have one week without a visit to the doctor
To enjoy life as I did in my youthful days
To see my name on someone's team roster

To be able to speak coherently about my past accomplishments
To speak of where I've been and whom I have met
To have that spark in my eye as I challenged life
To stay positive, happy and not sad

For, you see, I too was once young and quite active like you
Just ask around and those that know me will give me a good reference
I was on top of the world and did not have a care in the world
But time has taken its toll on me and that has been the difference

Enjoy life and safeguard memories because one day; the difference
    will be
Your youthful self will suddenly abandon you and you'll be just like
    me!

The Trip

Have you ever wondered how ones life is controlled by needs and not by necessity?
We have so much free time on our hands, yet we tend to accomplish very little
We cannot stay at home and do something beneficial or creative
We tend to go walk the mall or drink coffee at a local coffee shop or just piddle

We go from store to store and have no definite plan on what we are looking for
Our tendency is to walk and shop or try on some new and expensive clothing
The store clerks are anxious to help, but you decline their help basically saying
I am not really looking to buy I am just here killing time, just loafing

Ironically, this behavior is quite constant to an extent in each one of us
We just cannot stay home and read a book or watch a show on TV
Tend to think that we are bored and are missing out on something
Thus, the trip to the mall, a shopping center, or go drink some coffee

Just imagine for one minute that we would choose to invite our friend
To go to a local church, sit there, meditate, and ultimately just pray
You probably need to turn on your video on your smart phone and record a response
I am quite sure that friends will be taken aback and ask, "What did you just say?"

To most, church is not a fun place to go or to meet your friends just
to hang out
There is no excitement there and generally it is rude to carry a con-
versation inside a church
It's much more interesting to look at the new line of clothes or shoes
or jewelry
Better to window shop and gossip while walking or looking at a new
purse

No one will argue with you about your trip to the mall being more
pleasant than to a church
But where do you go if you need Divine Help if not to a church pew?
All of a sudden, the mall comes in second and you seek His help
And mingle with those at church, which generally are just a few

You see going to God's house can be full of rewards each and every
day
He is a very good listener, works miracles, and broken hearts He will
mend
So next time you get the urge to go spend some time away from
home
Remember He is there waiting for you, so go against the grain and
invite a friend

Keep in mind that Jesus said, "But lay up for yourselves treasures in
Heaven," where neither moth nor rust doth corrupt, and where
thieves do not break through nor steal
Now if you are fortunate, you do see and get extremely good sales at
the mall
But compared to what Jesus said, He offers us an extremely better deal

Food for thought and words to ponder
Where is the better deal?
Does this make you wonder?
Which do you choose—church or mall or a coffee shop for a sip?
Be different—go to church, invite your friends, and make the trip

Walk Away

I went to spend some time with mom and dad
I went to the place where they lay
I scolded myself for not being more of a caring son
And after cleaning their gravesite I, crying, walked away

I asked myself what would mom and dad do for me?
What would they do if I had been the one to pass away?
Would they visit me often and keep my gravesite clean?
Would they come to visit often and for me pray?

I know the answer to all my concerns and need not fear
For their love for me was genuine, real, and true
My grave would be clean and very well kept
I would have clean red roses and flowers—some purple and some
     blue

So I ask myself, why can't I do the same?
How much time is needed to clean their home?
To periodically place clean/fresh flowers on their grave?
To spend some time praying at their gravesite alone?

To shed a tear and tell them how much I miss them
To feel proud that their gravesite is clean and new flowers placed
     where they lay
To feel content that I am a truly caring son
To tell them that I'll be back soon and proudly walk away

And as I drive away, I take a final look and drive away a little sad
But I always say as I drive away—I'll always love you mom and dad!

Wanna Play Catch?

As a young man growing up, I had a very vivid imagination
Inspirations were abundant, but my aspirations were not hard to guess
I could hit the baseball a country mile and would play professional baseball
I would be another Pujols, Bonds, Griffey, Ryan, Clemens, and many, many more
I would be considered one of baseball's best

Everywhere I went and on every day of the week, you could see me
On the streets and people would say he is wearing the tools of the game he loves
I'd be sporting my best baseball cap slightly tilted to the right but pushed down to my ears
Baseball bat slung across my shoulder and baseball shirt tugged inside my shorts
It was not hard to notice my prized possession, which was my glove

I looked and walked like all my heroes past and present and never doubted I'd be like them
I'd grow up and make the big show and never, never forget about my past
The only problem that I had was that my illusionary mind could not make up its mind
Was I going to be an infielder, outfielder, catcher or pitcher or maybe just DH
I wanted to be an all-around player so picking only one did not last

Reality has a way of bringing you down to earth and to the present time

I would finally reach what I called a baseball field, which had no infield grass or lights

Matter of fact there were no base paths or bleachers and definitely no outfield fence

The place we called our home field was just that an old abandoned grass field

It was so big that you could not hit the ball to the road no matter if the ball was hit with all your might

There also were no teammates leastwise not enough to field a team

The town's population was small and the kids in school were even less

We only dreamt of wearing brand new baseball uniforms and competing against other towns

But we did not even have enough kids to compete against ourselves

Without practice, competition, or games it was going to be hard to be the best

But I had a secret weapon as my vivid imagination would always take the lead

I did not like to throw the baseball as far as I could cause then I'd have to fetch

I'd place my hand inside my old trusted glove and throw the baseball inside my glove

I'd repeat that action until I thought I was warm and ready to start

Would then look up to Heaven and ask Jesus—wanna play catch?

He never failed to show up for my practice and we threw for quite some time

He always appeared between the clouds and always, always smiled at me

He never seemed to tire and never lost His big and friendly smile

He never missed a ball I threw and always returned it down to me

Seems like I could hear Him say, "I'll always be here for thee"

I always heard my parents say that you have to learn from the best to
be the best
To study their ways and study how they act and what they do or say
But being in such a little town with no baseball team nor field
Was going to be hard for me to prosper and learn more than I already
knew
Another thing my parents would say is Jesus is the way

My parents never really knew that Jesus and I were on the same team
I was his favorite player and He always said I was the best player and
He was the last
He always encouraged me to never, never give up and to always
believe in myself and Him
To keep on practicing and coming to Him for our daily work outs in
baseball and in life
I now know that I did have a coach and mentor and was learning
from the best

My youth is now behind me but my vivid mind remains which is a
blessing to me
My baseball bat, cap, shoes, shorts, glove, and baseball are neatly
placed within a display bar
These items serve as a reminder of my past and of the great times I
had at practice
Of the great teammate I had and of all the teachings that He taught
and I learned
To believe in myself and confide and trust in Him as He would never
be far

You see, my dreams were not fully realized and I never made the big show
But I have no regrets as my adventurous and creative youth did not last
But who amongst you can honestly say that you had a better team-
mate than I?
Who can really say that your youthful time was well spent as you
learned?
Who can say that you spoke to Jesus and asked—you wanna play catch?

Was It Real?

Last night I had a wonderful and emotional dream.
I spoke to you, kissed you, and we stared lovingly at each other.
We shared so many happy and unforgettable moments.
You always knew how to make us smile be it husband, son, daughter, sister, or brother.

This dream was so real that I actually felt your hug, love, and kiss.
You always had a way of knowing what to say, do, or how to put others at ease.
Seeing and being with you and knowing that you are alright.
Made me relax and enjoy the moment—put me at peace.

I tried to tell you how much you are missed and show you my love.
But you touched my lips and told me to enjoy the moment we have together.
Told me that you also missed all your loved ones and feel their pain.
But life has to go on and that you will protect and love your family forever.

You spoke of the lessons in life that you taught your family.
To be strong, be patient, be persistent, and never, never give up.
To be tolerant, respectful, loving, decent, forgiving, humble, and nice.
To be faithful and when in need to say prayer to our God above

You also spoke about the hardships you and your family endured.
Used them as examples of the many trials you had to go through.

But I noticed your voice was wavering a bit and your eyes were watery too.
But you said, "My family made me strong just by constantly saying, 'Mom, I love you.'"

I want you to know and want you to tell all my family.
I have no regrets on how I treated my husband, daughters, and sons.
I showed you how to enjoy life and how to take care of your family.
I showed you no matter how difficult the trial—I showed you how to go on.

So with that said, I need you to speak to all my family and put them at ease.
To remember me, pray for me and to think only of the good we shared and lived.
To take care of each other as when I was with them, to be as happy as possible.
To comfort each other, live life lovingly, and for me not to constantly grieve.

Even though they may not see me as they did before or talk to me as before.
I still feel their sorrow and pain and their tears make me cry and make me sad
I love you so much and never liked to see you hurt or cry or to be without.
Remember my sickness and pain is gone—for that please be glad.

But before I leave as it looks like you are getting ready to wake up.
Tell my family to enjoy life and take care of their family like I used to do.
Be happy, make pleasant family moments, and keep me in their thoughts.
Laugh a lot, love a lot, and enjoy each other as like the time I spent with each of you.

What Will You Leave Behind?

As a child barely able to keep up with mom and dad
I'd trudge along and tried to keep in stride
But my stubby legs didn't allow me to increase my stride
But mom and dad were very tolerant and always said, "It's alright"

I walked beside them like I owned the world and everything else
I had no fear walking besides my mom and dad
I didn't like it when they tried to hold my hand
They knew not to try because it made me real mad

I was a big boy and had my own way of thinking
Totally independent and could take care of myself
My mom and dad used to smile because they knew otherwise
Because I always had mom give me the peanut butter way up on the
    shelf

My dad had a way of talking and had that powerful manly look
He'd wave at his friends and sometimes would firmly shake their
    hand
I studied his manners and mimicked his laughter
I was going to be like my dad—kept studying and saying I can

I looked at my mom and couldn't understand
How this smaller woman had total control of our home
She'd sometimes get mad at dad and let him know where he stood
She was tough, direct just like the biggest dog that always had the bone

But come Sunday morning dad and I had better be ready on time
There was a church service that we definitely had to attend

We wore our best clothes that mom had made ready for us
Jesus was our Savior—but in our house mom was the boss—amen

I watched both my parents as the church service commenced
I noticed that both of them were moving their lips while praying to
    God
They sat very still and hardly, hardly ever moved
But if I tried to look around, both my parents gave me a negative nod

It's been quite some time since I scurried along with mom and dad
As I have grown up and have a family of my own
I have a son that reminds me so much of me in my youth
Walks with his head high, chest puffed like he was full-grown

And I also remember and now realize that moms are the backbone
    of any home
Do something against the grain and see who applies discipline
And it does not matter whether it was her child or her husband
When she's mad we'd better be still, attentive and listen

It's ironic how we remember our youthful years
Tracking along and really proud to be with mom and dad
Remembering how they took special care of me
Such memories make me smile and make me real glad

I am sure that they knew that someday I'd reminisce about my youth
Think of the happy times and would grow up and follow their lead
Lead by example and do and say the right thing
Firmly shake a friend's hand, just like dad, wherever I meet

You see, time may pass and the world has a way of changing
Things that were may no longer be with us except what is good or bad
But the choice is easy for me and for my wife and son
We will make the right choice because that was our training from
    mom and dad

Who Caught Who

As a youngster I'd always roam the fields.
Always running after grasshoppers, always trying to catch one.
But this morning was no different than the day before.
Plenty of grasshoppers everywhere, but I had caught none.

It seemed like they knew I was coming and let me get real close.
But just as I was about to catch one, he'd always fly away.
It was a silly game we played and one where I always lost.
But the grasshoppers would be there, waiting for me the following day.

But this special morning, I had come up with a very good plan.
I planned to roam the fields and pretend I was only playing there.
Maybe the grasshoppers would not be afraid of me.
And stay put when I got real close instead of flying everywhere.

My plan seemed to work as the grasshoppers let me get real close.
Several times, it seems like I could just reach out and catch one.
But just when I thought that my plan was really, really working.
I tried to catch many grasshoppers, but in the end I had none

I was mad at myself for not being able to catch a grasshopper.
I laid down in the field and thought—maybe I need to catch some-
    thing without wings.
I started thinking of what I could catch that didn't have wings.
If it didn't fly, then catching them should be a simple thing.

I was still thinking of what I could chase and finally catch.
When I saw a butterfly flying low and slow above the grass.

The game was on, and I was up to catching this floating butterfly.
The challenge was set, and I felt that this challenge I would pass

No sooner did I jump up to catch this butterfly flying so low.
That I realized I had moved too quick and way too fast.
The butterfly saw me and quickly moved its wings.
Flew straight up, way, way above the grass.

But strange as it may seem and still I wonder.
The butterfly flew above me and never went away.
I kept looking at the pretty colors on the butterfly's wings.
And kept thinking, maybe this is my lucky day

I placed my arms above my head and opened my hand.
And spoke to the butterfly like it would understand.
I told the butterfly that I would not hurt it or her wings
And that on my hand or finger it could land.

It's strange to say what really happened on that day.
But the butterfly did float back down and landed on my hand.
As I brought my hand slowly downward I kept on talking to the
    butterfly.
Reassuring it that I only wanted to see it up close—if only I can.

It seemed like the butterfly knew what I was saying.
As it had wrapped its arms around my finger and was looking closely
    at me.
I also was looking at this very pretty and colorful butterfly.
Thinking that when I told this story—no one would believe me

We studied each other it seemed like for many, many days.
But in reality it was only minutes—only minutes and only a few.
But as I let the butterfly fly away unharmed.
I watched it float away and thought, who caught who?

Who Was the Blind One?

Many moons ago, as I sat on park bench feeling totally worthless and dejected, I was surprised when an older man asked for permission to sit next to me. I did not look at the older gentleman, so I could not tell you what he looked like or what he was wearing much less where he came from. I just acknowledged with hand gestures that part of the bench was his to take.

I heard and felt when the man sat down, and he commenced to talk to me and started telling me things that he should not have known. He mentioned my heartache over losing my loved one and that he could tell that I was very upset and miserable. Said that I should pray to God for the departed soul of my loved one. Told me that God would hear my prayers and help me heal.

Once he finished talking about my loss, he turned to me and told me that I had turned away from God because God does not listen nor help. I looked away ashamed and awestruck that this man knew this fact about me. How did he know? Who was he? Where did he come from? Man went on to say that God is patient and is waiting for me to come back, and that deep down, I wanted to go back to my Lord and God. The man was right, but still, I would not look at this person.

Man went on to tell me that my loved one had suffered so much, but that I had suffered much more. Told me that when my wife told me that she loved me and forgave me for all the wrongs I thought I had done, that she really meant it. How did he know that? My wife did have that conversation with me.

This person went on to tell me about how bad I felt for our two sons and one daughter. That I was thinking how was life going to be without their mom? Told me that my children needed me now more than ever, and that I needed to take them to church and God and pray for family unity, support, and strength. Told me that I was the father and needed to act like one.

Finally, he told me that I needed to keep my job and quit thinking of leaving. Reminded me to be a father to our kids and that involved buying them clothes, food, and other basic necessities. How did he know I was thinking of quitting my job?

I was starting to get concerned about this person knowing so much about me that I turned and faced him. I was set back when I noticed that this person was blind. This person was blind, yet he could see my pain and could see my thoughts. How?

I asked this person how he knew what he knew about me? How could you know and see so much when you are blind? His answer startled me when he answered, "Yes, I am blind, but you have eyes, but do not see, you have ears, but do not hear." Went on to say that, in his blindness, he has to be able to hear the faintest sound and to detect emotions of others. He said I was a lot more blind than he was because even in his blindness, he sought God and visited God in His house. I, on the other hand, was running away from Him when I needed Him the most.

I left that park bench a new person, went straight home, hugged my kids, and took them for a ride. Rode right over to the church where my wife and I were married. Spoke to the pastor, and he prayed over us for family unity, support, and strength—just like the blind man said, so that we could pass through this very hard and troubling time.

It took a blind man to show me the Christian path to life, and for that I am truly grateful. How many of you need a visit from a blind person to get you going the right Christian way? Now is the time to seek and find God and to stay with Him no matter what.

Why?

I magine if the good Lord would intentionally blind the prejudiced person ... and once blind, would this person ask for a drink of water and take the cup of water from a person that he feels is inferior. Would he say, "Thank you," upon quenching his thirst? And after drinking and regaining his sight, would he be a different person?

Can you judge the goodness of a person by his color/race? Can you touch a person's hand and discern his color/race? If you were drowning, would you see the color of the hand trying to help before grasping that hand? Would you look at skin color if a person tries to help you financially? When you get to the pearly gate do you know the color of the person controlling the gate?

Why Did You Stay Away?

Where were you when I needed to talk?
When I needed to reminisce about our youthful days?
Why did you not come to see me when I was in need?
Why did we not get together to cry, laugh and pray?

I missed you so much and needed you by my side.
To strengthen me and cry with me and make me smile!
To hold my hand and reassure me that all was all right!
I would have been content if you only stayed a while!

Where did I go wrong and where did we stray apart?
Was it something I said or did or even failed to do?
If that was the reason, you should have confided in me
I would have apologized and said, "I really do love you"

It's funny how time takes its toll on all of us.
How, as youngsters, we fought and could not get along.
But, as we age, we tend to mellow and our eyes and heart get soft.
And, all of a sudden, my family cannot do me any wrong.

I left without really saying the proper goodbye
I wish I could have kissed you and said, "I love you," as we prayed.
But it's okay as I forgive you and will say, "I loved you all to the end."
But next time I see you, I will ask you, "Why did you stay away?"

About the Author

As a young kid growing up in deep south Texas, I always had an interest in poetry. Poetry was a communication outlet for me. Now, at the ripe old age of sixty-eight, I am still fascinated by poetry. Inspirations come to me at different times during the day, but most inspirations come to me while I am asleep. When I get an inspiration, I can create a whole poem in my head. Once I get up from bed and log onto my computer, I, in most cases, can have a finished copy or first draft within minutes. Some of the poems that I have submitted here did not take me long to create. My wife, Dolores, would tell me, "There is no way you could have made that poem so quickly." But I have done them all fairly quick. I might not have written my poem as dreamt, but end product is real close if not identical to inspiration.

My favorite subject in high school was English class. Here I read for the first time a poem by Joyce Kilmer titled, "Trees." This is still one of my favorite poems. I guess Joyce said it best in so far as all of us want to be poets when he wrote, "Poems are made by fools like me. But only God can make a tree." Powerful words!

I attended Mission High School where I participated on our high school football, baseball, and track teams respectively. In high school and my earlier years, I was a gifted athlete. God had given me enough talent in sports to be considered one of the best players on our baseball or football team—and enough talent to go to Pan American University on a baseball scholarship. Our university baseball team is and forever will be the only baseball team from this university to go to and compete in the NCAA Baseball World Series in Omaha, Nebraska. I say that because this certain university has changed its name and also its mascot.

But through it all, I was infatuated with writing whether it was creating songs, writing policies, or procedures for work processes or my profound love for creating poetry. I truly hope that some of these poems written are telling of one of your life's experiences.

My hope though is that these poems or stories bring out the goodness within each of us, and we start seeing less fortunate Christian brothers and sisters in a much different and positive light. Their struggles are real, their heartaches are constant, but their devotion to their special needs child or children is genuine and truly commendable. Take time to visit with one of these individuals, and you will be inwardly gratified at their resilience and strength, not to mention their faith.

Thank you for the purchase of this book, hope you enjoyed and were inwardly moved while reading a poem or two. May your blessings be many!

Keep in mind that special needs children and the parents of these angels are humans that need love, support, and encouragement. Interact with these individuals wherever seen, and I am sure that if you do this with an open and positive mind that you will enjoy the interaction as much as the special needs child or parents!

God's blessings!

CPSIA information can be obtained
at www.ICGtesting.com
Printed in the USA
BVHW061235180319
542952BV00033B/2844/P